THE

EVERYTHING KIDS'

Animal Puzzle & Activity Book

Slither, Soar, and Swing Through a Jungle of Fun!

By Beth L. Blair and Jennifer A. Ericsson

Adams Media

Avon, Massachusetts

EDITORIAL
Publishing Director: Gary M. Krebs
Managing Editor: Kate McBride
Copy Chief: Laura M. Daly
Acquisitions Editor: Kate Burgo
Production Editors: Bridget Brace, Jamie Wielgus

PRODUCTION
Production Director: Susan Beale
Production Manager: Michelle Roy Kelly
Series Designers: Colleen Cunningham, Erin Ring
Layout and Graphics: Colleen Cunningham, Rachael Eiben, John Paulhus, Daria Perreault, Erin Ring
Cover Layout: Paul Beatrice, Matt LeBlanc

An Everything® Series Book.
Everything® and everything.com® are registered trademarks of F+W Publications, Inc.

Published by Adams Media, an F+W Publications Company
57 Littlefield Street, Avon, MA 02322. U.S.A.
www.adamsmedia.com
ISBN 10: 1-59337-305-8
ISBN 13: 978-1-59337-305-4

Printed in the United States of America.

J I H G F E D C B

This publication is designed to provide accurate and authoritative information with regard to the subject matter covered. It is sold with the understanding that the publisher is not engaged in rendering legal, accounting, or other professional advice. If legal advice or other expert assistance is required, the services of a competent professional person should be sought.
—From a *Declaration of Principles* jointly adopted by a Committee of the American Bar Association and a Committee of Publishers and Associations

Many of the designations used by manufacturers and sellers to distinguish their products are claimed as trademarks. When those designations appear in this book and Adams Media was aware of a trademark claim, the designations have been printed with initial capital letters.

Cover illustrations by Dana Regan.
Interior illustrations by Kurt Dolber.
Puzzles by Beth L. Blair.

This book is available at quantity discounts for bulk purchases.
For information, please call 1-800-289-0963.

See the entire Everything® series at *www.everything.com.*

Contents

DEDICATION

*From Beth and Jenny, to all the animals we have loved
(but especially Ester and Wheezer).*

Introduction

The world is full of wild and wonderful creatures. Some live on land, some live in the ocean, and some live in your house. Some animals fly, some slither, some swim, and some can run as fast as your mom or dad can drive a car! Each animal is fascinating—and we've tried to create puzzles that represent the uniqueness in all of them.

It was impossible for us to fit all the animals of the world into the pages of this book. There are more than a million different species of just insects! That's three times as many species as all the other kinds of animals put together! But we did try hard to include a wide variety of the biggest, the fastest, the most beloved, and the most interesting.

We also tried to offer you many different types of puzzles. There are mazes and word searches, codes and hidden pictures, acrostics and math puzzles, dot-to-dots and criss-crosses. To give you a little taste of what's inside, see if you can find the hidden words in this word search that all describe A-N-I-M-A-L-S. Hint: There is one word for each letter.

```
L T H E R E A R S E O
I N A T U R A L U V E
V R M F O U R T P H O
I U A W E S O M E S A
N N Z D S P E C R I E
G N I T S E R E T N I
S O N F M A M M A L S
M A G N I F I C E N T
```

EXTRA FUN: After you have found the seven hidden words, read the leftover letters from top to bottom and left to right. They will spell out an amazing animal fact!

The Everything® Kids' Animal Puzzle & Activity Book is divided into nine sections. Most chapters focus on animal habitats like the Arctic or the rainforest, but the book wouldn't be complete without a section on our favorite pets and a careful look at endangered species.

We hope you have a great time with the puzzles, but we also hope that you'll come away from this book with a greater appreciation for the many species that surround us. We certainly did!

Happy Puzzling,
Beth L. Blair and Jennifer A. Ericsson

P.S. Remember to look for Mervin the mouse—he's hidden on every puzzle page!

Extra Extra Fun: Use your favorite crayons to color in all the chapter openers!!

Chapter 1

Arctic Animals

Cold Creatures Criss-Cross

Even though the Arctic is one of the coldest places in the world, there are animals that live there year-round. Can you fit all of the Arctic residents from the word list into the grid? We've left some chilly words to get you started!

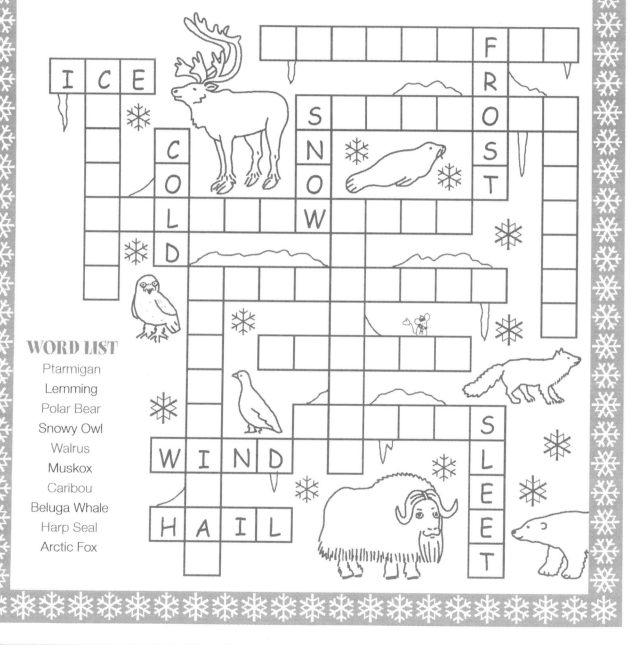

WORD LIST

Ptarmigan
Lemming
Polar Bear
Snowy Owl
Walrus
Muskox
Caribou
Beluga Whale
Harp Seal
Arctic Fox

Where Are We?

Color in all the penguins that have X, Y, or Z on them.

Read the remaining letters from left to right, top to bottom to get the answer to this riddle:

What do you call a colony of penguins living in the Arctic?

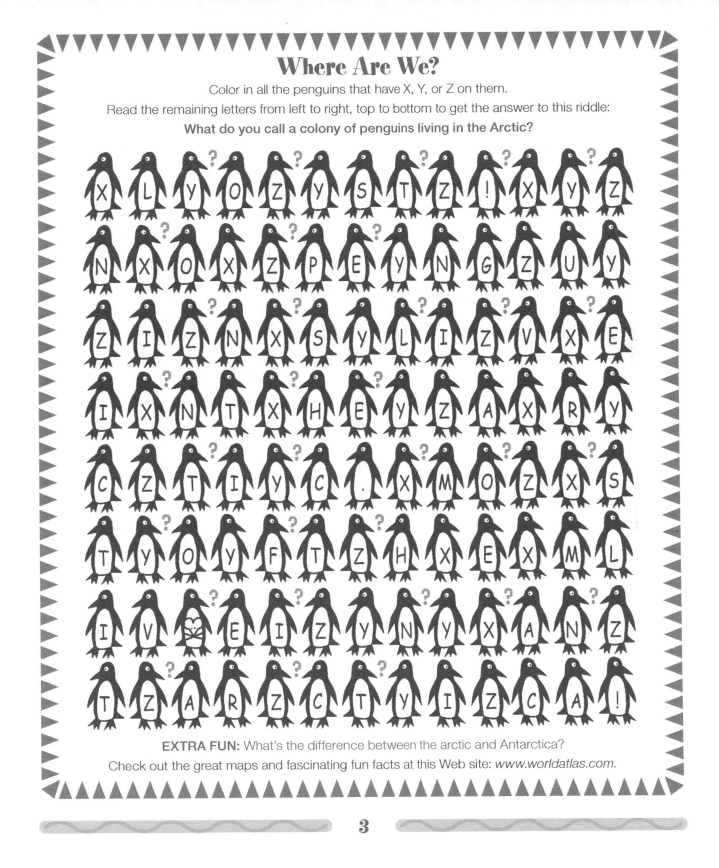

EXTRA FUN: What's the difference between the arctic and Antarctica?

Check out the great maps and fascinating fun facts at this Web site: *www.worldatlas.com.*

White in Winter

Many arctic animals like the ptarmigan, arctic fox, and arctic hare turn white in the winter to blend in with the snow. They do this to avoid their predators. Break the code in the boxes below. Fill in the letters to learn the special word for this survival technique.

	E-2	first	N-1	L+3	T+1	sixth	O-3	first	H-1	D+1

Where's the Fox?

This is a picture of an arctic fox in a snow storm! However, during the summer, the arctic fox's fur becomes darker. To see what he looks like in warm weather, use a brown crayon or colored pencil to fill in each box that has a small dot in the upper right-hand corner.

The arctic fox is only as big as a large house cat!

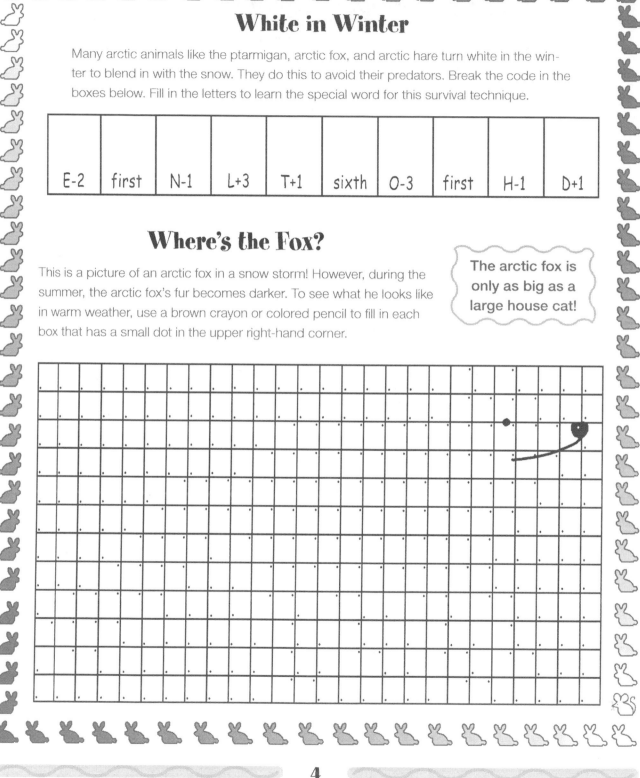

Polar Bear Treats

Each of these scrambled words is something a polar bear likes to eat.
Unscramble them and read the circled letters from top to bottom. They
will spell out a polar bear's very favorite food!

1. M A L O N S = ⓪ _ _ _ _ _

2. S R I B E E R = _ _ _ _ _ ⓪ _

3. R A L S W U = _ ⓪ _ _ _ _

4. M I G N E L M S = ⓪ _ _ _ _ _ _ _

5. G E S G = _ _ _ ⓪

Totally Cool

Animals that live in the arctic are very hardy!
They are able to survive long periods of dark-
ness and freezing cold. Five words that mean
the same thing as "cold" are hidden in this grid.
To find them, take one letter from each column moving from
left to right. Each letter can only be used once, so cross
them off as you use them. The first word is done for you.

C	R	O	G	T	Y
F	R	I	S	E	D
F	I	N	L	R	Y
W	H	I	T	L	N
F	R	O	Z	I	Y

1. CHILLY
2. _____
3. _____
4. _____
5. _____

What's a "Whale-Horse"?

It is the Norwegian name for a big arctic animal with thick, wrinkled skin, flippers, and long ivory tusks. To discover the more familiar name for this creature, start at number 1 and connect all the dots.

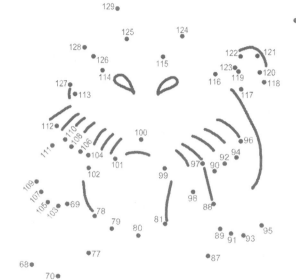
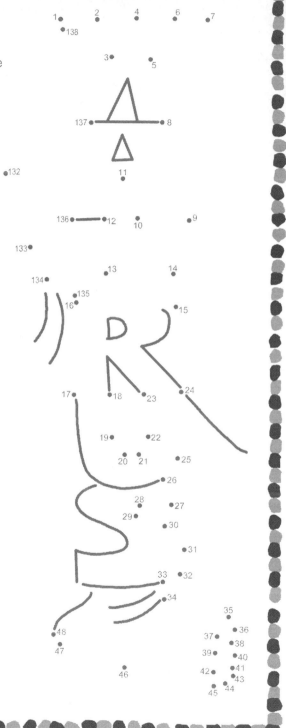

Common Cold

Polar bears and caribou may look very different, but they have something in common that helps them to survive their arctic environment! Answer as many clues below as you can. Fill the letters into the grid. Work back and forth between the clues and the grid until you get the answer to this question:

What is it that helps both polar bears and caribou keep in body heat and stay afloat in water?

1D	2E	3G	4E		5A B	6D	7F	8G		9B	10 A A	11 C	12 C	
13 F	14 G	15 H	16 H	17 D	18 E		19 C	20 A A	21 B	22 G	23 C			
24 F	25 B		26 D	27 D	28 B	29 H	30 C		31 B	32 F	33 B	34 C	35 E	36 G

A. The sound a sheep makes

$$\frac{B}{5} \quad \frac{A}{20} \quad \frac{A}{10}$$

B. Not in front of

$$\frac{}{31} \quad \frac{}{28} \quad \frac{}{9} \quad \frac{}{21} \quad \frac{}{25} \quad \frac{}{33}$$

C. What your body does when it's cold

$$\frac{}{23} \quad \frac{}{19} \quad \frac{}{34} \quad \frac{}{11} \quad \frac{}{12} \quad \frac{}{30}$$

D. One of the things you chew with

$$\frac{}{1} \quad \frac{}{17} \quad \frac{}{6} \quad \frac{}{26} \quad \frac{}{27}$$

E. Curds and _____

$$\frac{}{18} \quad \frac{}{2} \quad \frac{}{35} \quad \frac{}{4}$$

F. Sound an owl makes

$$\frac{}{13} \quad \frac{}{32} \quad \frac{}{24} \quad \frac{}{7}$$

G. Land at the edge of water

$$\frac{}{36} \quad \frac{}{8} \quad \frac{}{14} \quad \frac{}{22} \quad \frac{}{3}$$

H. Sick

$$\frac{}{29} \quad \frac{}{15} \quad \frac{}{16}$$

Mighty Muskox

Figure out where to put each of the scrambled letters in the puzzle grid, below. They all fit in spaces under their own column. When you have correctly filled in the grid, you will have the answer to this mighty mystery:

When a herd of muskox are threatened, how do they react?

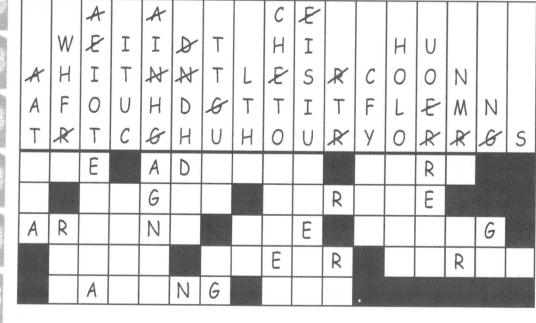

Caribou Moves

As the seasons change, this herd of caribou moves from the forest to the tundra, looking for food. Can you find your way through the herd? Pick up the letters along the way to spell out the nine-letter word for this seasonal wandering.

Close Up

Oops! Our wildlife photographer got his finger frozen to his camera's zoom lens. Can you tell what arctic animal is in each close-up picture? Match each photo to an animal name from the list. Not all names are used. Write the number under the picture.

1. Snowy Owl
2. Walrus
3. Polar Bear
4. Muskox
5. Caribou
6. Seal

Polar Playroom

A mother polar bear digs a den in the snow where she will have her babies and take care of them for several months. She often digs a playroom so her cubs will have room to move around. This mother bear seems to have gotten carried away with her digging! Can you show the cubs the way back to their mother?

START

END

Flippered Family

Walruses and seals both belong to a group of arctic mammals that have flippers. To learn the funny name of this flippered family, finish these sentences about walruses and seals. Then fill the correct letters into the numbered spaces.

They swim in the $\underset{1}{\_\_}\ \underset{2}{\_\_}\ \underset{3}{T}\ \underset{4}{E}\ \underset{5}{\_\_}$.

They breathe $\underset{6}{\_\_}\ \underset{7}{\_\_}\ \underset{8}{\_\_}$.

They rest on $\underset{9}{\_\_}\ \underset{10}{\_\_}\ \underset{11}{N}\ \underset{12}{\_\_}$.

$\underset{13}{\_\_}\ \underset{14}{O}\ \underset{15}{\_\_}\ \underset{16}{\_\_}\ \underset{17}{\_\_}\quad \underset{18}{\_\_}\ \underset{19}{E}\ \underset{20}{\_\_}\ \underset{21}{\_\_}\ \underset{22}{S}$ hunt them.

Their babies drink $\underset{23}{\_\_}\ \underset{24}{\_\_}\ \underset{25}{L}\ \underset{26}{\_\_}$.

Blubber keeps them $\underset{27}{W}\ \underset{28}{\_\_}\ \underset{29}{\_\_}\ \underset{30}{\_\_}$.

Flippered Family Name
$\underset{13}{\_\_}\ \underset{24}{\_\_}\ \underset{11}{\_\_}\ \underset{11}{\_\_}\ \underset{7}{\_\_}\ \underset{13}{\_\_}\ \underset{4}{\_\_}\ \underset{12}{\_\_}$

Solve the math problems swimming around the edge of this page. Write the matching letters on the correct lines below to answer the riddle.

What's a perfect pinniped?
$\underset{8}{\_\_}\ \underset{3}{\_\_}\quad \underset{1}{\_\_}\ \underset{9}{\_\_}\ \underset{5}{\_\_}\ \underset{8}{\_\_}\ \underset{2}{\_\_}\quad \underset{6}{\_\_}\ \underset{5}{\_\_}\ \underset{8}{\_\_}\ \underset{2}{\_\_}$

(Border problems: N $1+1+1$, I $0+4-3$, S $2+3+1$, D $10+5-6$, L $10-3-5$, E $4+1-1$, A $3+6-1$)

11

From May to September, one pair of snowy owls must catch thousands of lemmings to feed themselves and their chicks!

Lots of Lemmings

Lemmings are arctic rodents about the size of a guinea pig. They are a snowy owl's favorite food. Can you find the 11 times the word "LEMMING" is hiding in this picture of a snowy owl and her hungry chick?

How Many Buses Equal One Shark?

The whale shark is the biggest fish in the ocean, weighing up to 15 tons! But how big is that really? Use the "How Many Buses?" formula to figure out how much a whale shark weighs in more familiar terms.

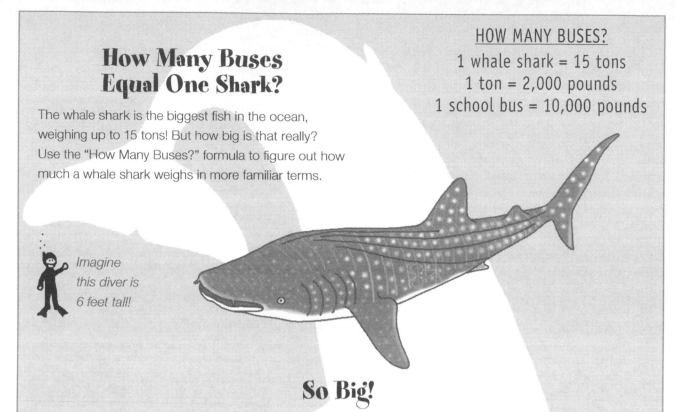

Imagine this diver is 6 feet tall!

So Big!

There's another ocean animal that's even bigger than a whale shark. In fact, this creature is bigger than any other animal on land or sea, including the biggest dinosaur that ever lived! Use the directions to cross words out of the grid. Read the remaining words from left to right and top to bottom.

Cross out all words . . .

. . . that mean "small"
. . . that rhyme with "fin"
. . . that start with the letter "D"
. . . that end in "-ing"
. . . with two letters, one of which is "A"
. . . that rhyme with "big"
. . . with double "OO"

SING	THE	DOLPHIN	PIN	LARGEST
FIG	LITTLE	ANIMAL	AT	WOOD
ON	EARTH	COOL	DOWN	JIG
NOODLE	TOO	WIN	IS	TINY
THE	POOL	HOOT	BRING	DIVE
SOON	DEEP	BLUE	PIG	WIG
WING	TIN	AM	WHALE	FOOL

EXTRA FUN: This biggest-of-creatures can weigh up to 220 tons! Use the "How Many Buses" formula to see how many school buses that equals!

Water World

There are more than 24,000 different species of fish living in the waters of the world! Can you find all the fish swimming in the grid? One has been highlighted for you. When you are done, read the unused letters from left to right and top to bottom to discover just how much of the earth is a water covered habitat.

EXTRA FUN:

Try using a light blue marker or crayon to run a single line of color through each name. It will make the final answer much more interesting!

```
B  G  P  C  B  A  S  S  A  E  T  S  M  O  R  E  T  H
A  S  O  R  O        B  K  N  H  S  A  N  T  W  O  T
R  S  T  B  A  D  A  I  U  T  O  C  H  I  R  D  S  O
R  T  H  I  I  C  P  R  N  L  R  A  F  T  H  E  S  U
A  E  U  A  C  E  G  A  E  E  E  T  R  F  A  C  E  O
C  T  H     D  K  C  S  R  E  O  F  F  T  H  E  E  A
U  R  E  A  S  A  L  P  K  A  S  I  R  T  H  I  S  C
D  A  N  H  L  T  T  E  E  A  Y  S  O  V  E  R  E  D
A  U  A  E  L        R  B  R  T  H  W  I  T  H  W  A
T  R  O  E  W  A  H  O  O  A  C  E  T  E  R  T  H  A
K  C  M  A  N  G  L  E  R  U  C  H  T  S  H  O  W  M
   S  M  A  C  K  E  R  E  L  T  K  U  C  H  O  F  T
S  T  U  R  G  E  O  N  Y  W  T  M  H  I  S  P  U  Z
A  H  E  R  R  I  N  G  N  R  E  I  Z  L  E  I  S  C
L  Y  E  R  P  M  A  L  N  A  L  N  O  V  E  R  E  D
M  S  A  R  D  I  N  E  E  S  L  N  W  I  T  H  T  H
O  A  H  N  A  R  I  P  L  S  U  O  E  N  A  M  E  S
N  G  R  O  U  P  E  R  B  E  M  W  O  F  F  I  S  H
```

ABA
ANGLER
BARRACUDA
BASS
BLENNY
CARP
CATFISH
COD
COELACANTHS
EEL
GOBIE
GROUPER
GRUNT
HERRING
LAMPREY
MACKEREL
MINNOW
MULLET
NEHU
OREOS
PERCH
PIKE
PIRANHA
RAY
SALMON
SARDINE
SHAD
SHARK
SKATE
SMELT
SOLE
STICKLEBACK
STURGEON
TETRA
TROUT
TUNA
WAHOO
WRASSE

15

Create a Fish

Some of these names of real fish might give you ideas of how to draw silly fish! Use the shapes provided to start your drawings. Color your fish when finished!

PARROTFISH
CLOWNFISH
TRUMPETFISH
PENCILFISH
FLAGTAIL
DOTTYBACK

1.

2.

3.

Crusty Fellow

Look closely at the plants in this picture. They will tell you the silly answer to this unlikely question:

Why wouldn't the lobster share his toys?

START

Army of Arms

Each of these four creatures has a head surrounded by tentacles or arms. While an octopus has only eight, a nautilus can have more than eighty! Can you make it from START to END through this grasping group without getting caught?

E 2

T 8

Octopus

D 10

Squid

E 9

D 1 H

O 7

A 3

D 4

Funny Family

These creatures all belong to a family with an odd, but descriptive, name. What is it? Break the letter code and find out! Write your answer on the lines provided.

Cuttlefish

O 6

F 5

Nautilus

These creatures belong to the

_ _ _ _ - _ _ _ _ _ family.

END

Nice Neigh-bor

What ocean animal has a snout like a trumpet, a pouch like a kangaroo, and a grasping tail like a monkey? Copy the pattern in each numbered square into the proper place in the grid, and you will find out!

Lights, Please!

Most sea creatures live in water that is warmed by the sun. But some live deep in the sea where it is cold and dark. Creatures who live down there must make their own light! Use a white gel pen to connect the dots from 1 to 99 and you will see a very strange deep-ocean fish.

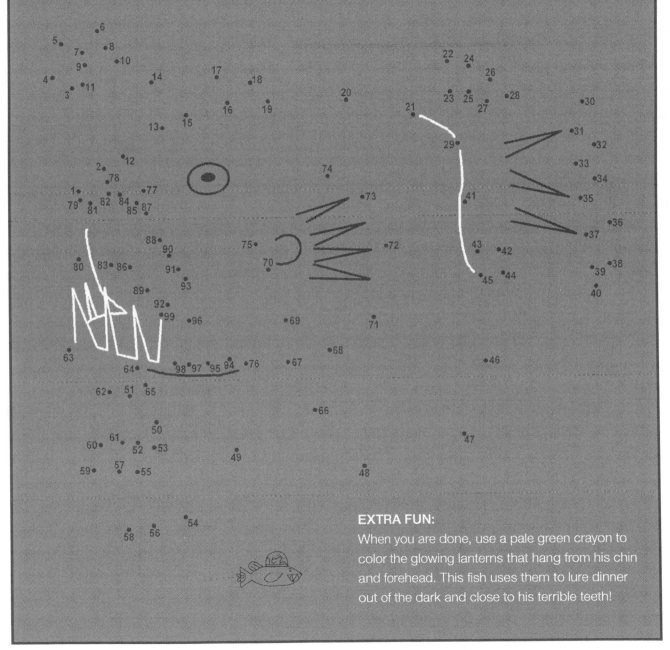

EXTRA FUN:

When you are done, use a pale green crayon to color the glowing lanterns that hang from his chin and forehead. This fish uses them to lure dinner out of the dark and close to his terrible teeth!

Ocean Hink Pinks

The answers to hink pinks are two rhyming words that each have one syllable. We've provided you with one of the words for each answer in the word list. Figure out which word goes where, and think of another word to complete each hink pink. **HINT:** One is done for you!

1. What a gilled water animal wants = <u>F I S H</u> <u>W I S H</u>
2. Letters to a large ocean mammal = _ _ _ _ _ _ _ _ _
3. Little tiny body of water = _ _ _ _ _ _
4. A great home for a hermit crab = _ _ _ _ _ _ _ _ _ _
5. Where fish with sharp teeth play = _ _ _ _ _ _ _ _ _
6. Flippered sea animal's food = _ _ _ _ _ _ _ _
7. Genuine snake-like fish = _ _ _ _ _ _ _ _
8. Metal fish part = _ _ _ _ _ _
9. Slow moving bunch of mollusks = _ _ _ _ _ _ _
10. Flat shark relative that likes sunlight = _ _ _ _ _ _

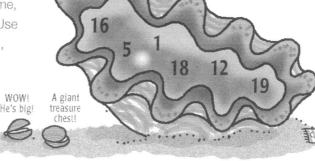

Hey! You have a PALE TAIL!

Very funny!

DAY JAM REAL SWELL MAIL WEE ~~WISH~~ PARK MEAL TIN

Hidden Treasure

Giant blue clams can grow over a yard wide and can live for 100 years! Over time, they can produce something valuable. Use a simple number substitution code (A=1, B=2, C=3 . . .) to find out what that is.

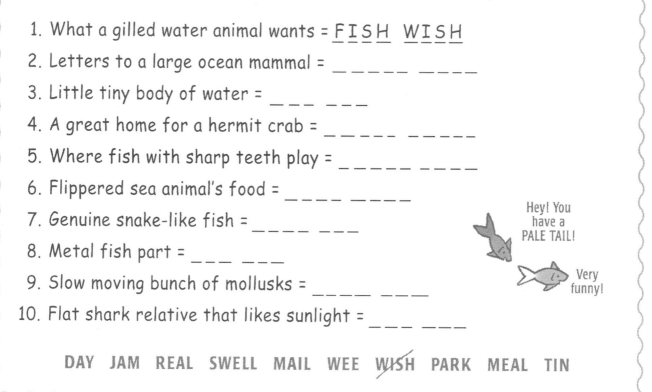

16 5 1 18 12 19

WOW! He's big!

A giant treasure chest!

Where's Dinner?

"Toothed whales" have sharp teeth that they use to catch a tasty dinner of fish or squid. But first they have to find their food! These whales send out a special kind of sound, and listen for the echoes that bounce back to them. These three whales have each sent out a sound.

ADD the numbers in the shaded path from the whale to the fish.
SUBTRACT the numbers on the unshaded path on the way back.

The whale with the lowest number is closest to eating dinner. He's the winner!

Narwhal

3 3 1 4 3
2 1 4
2 1 1
1
2 9
3 6
3 1
1 2

Beluga

1
3
2 3
1 3
7 2
9 2
9 3
1 4 3
4 1
3 1 3 3
1 3 3
1 2 2
2 1 1
1 1

What did the
sperm whale say
to the dolphin who
splashed him?

1 2 2 3 1 4 7 6 1 4 3
1 7 1 2 3 6 3 1 1 2 1

You did that
on porpoise!

killer whale

Who's a Whale?

There is a very familiar ocean mammal that you will be surprised to find is a toothed whale. Add the missing lines to spell his name!

Blue Baby

One kind of ocean baby is born blue or gray to blend in with the dark ocean. But this baby looks very different when it grows up! Use a dark crayon to fill in all the boxes with a dot in the upper left-hand corner. To break the letter-shifting code, fill in the letters either one before or one after the letters shown. Which is it?

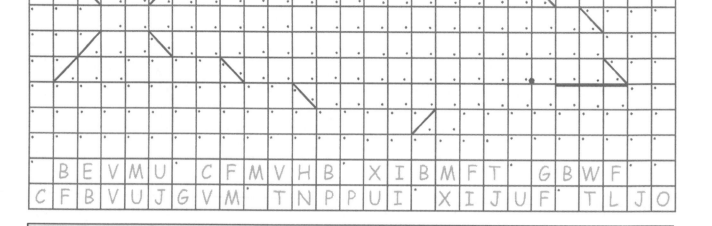

| B | E | V | M | U | | C | F | M | V | H | B | | X | I | B | M | F | T | | G | B | W | F | |
| C | F | B | V | U | J | G | V | M | | T | N | P | P | U | I | | X | I | J | U | F | | T | L | J | O |

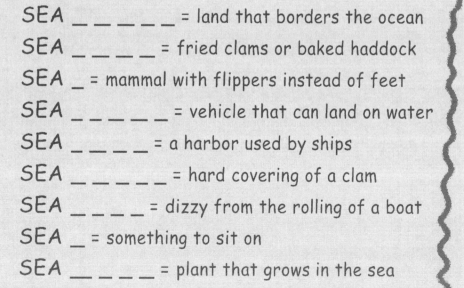

What Do You Sea?

How many "sea" words do you know? Finish each word by writing the correct letters on the dotted lines provided.

SEA _ _ _ _ _ = land that borders the ocean

SEA _ _ _ _ = fried clams or baked haddock

SEA _ = mammal with flippers instead of feet

SEA _ _ _ _ _ = vehicle that can land on water

SEA _ _ _ _ = a harbor used by ships

SEA _ _ _ _ _ = hard covering of a clam

SEA _ _ _ _ = dizzy from the rolling of a boat

SEA _ = something to sit on

SEA _ _ _ _ _ = plant that grows in the sea

At the Shore

Not all ocean animals live in the deep sea. Many of them can be found at the shore, where the land meets the water. How many of each animal can you find in this picture? **HINT:** Some animals are where you might expect to find them, and some are hiding in unexpected places. Don't forget to look for Mervin!

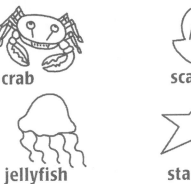

crab

scallop

jellyfish

starfish

Home Sweet Habitat

Where the ocean water is clear, warm, and shallow, special places have formed that attract a variety of colorful sea life. Fit the creatures listed below into their proper place up and down in the grid. Read across the shaded row to learn what this wonderful habitat is called. We left you a M-A-N-T-A R-A-Y to show you the way!

SPONGE, SEA ANEMONE, SHRIMP, ANGELFISH, OCTOPUS,
SEAHORSE, CLOWNFISH, HERMIT CRAB, JELLYFISH

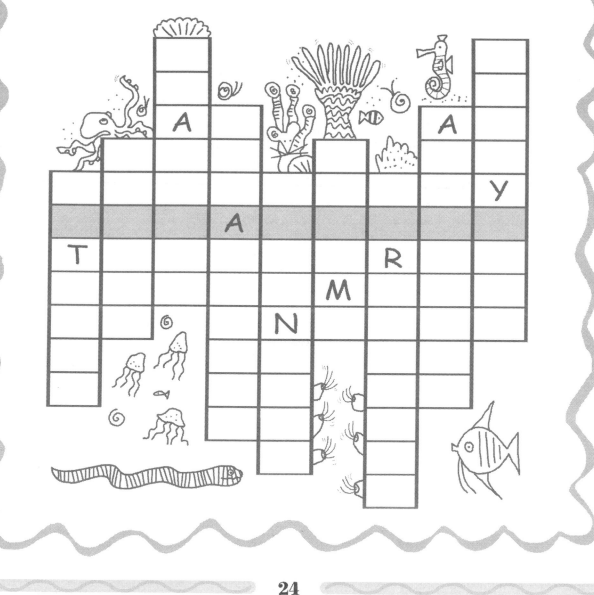

Chapter 3

Mountain and Woodland Animals

Scrambled Eggs

A hungry grizzly bear will eat almost anything—and a lot of it! Unscramble these words, which are all favorite bear foods. Then, try to fit the food items into the criss-cross. We've left some B-E-A-R F-O-O-D to get you started.

AGRSS_____

AVELES_____

GSEG_____

TANS_____

OTROS_____

UIRRSQEL_____

OWEFLRS_____

NEHOY_____

EDER_____

RBHES_____

RRIBEES_____

SOBIN_____

PHEGORS_____

LBBUS_____

ZALIRD_____

LMOSAN_____

RBAGAGE_____

Fit this word into the criss-cross, too:
—CARRION—
Do you know what it is?
Read the secret message to find out!

ROTTEN MEAT

A Mountain What?

The Mountain Goat is not really a goat at all. To find out what type of animal it is, find the correct path up the mountain from START to END. The letters on the rocks along the way will spell out the answer.

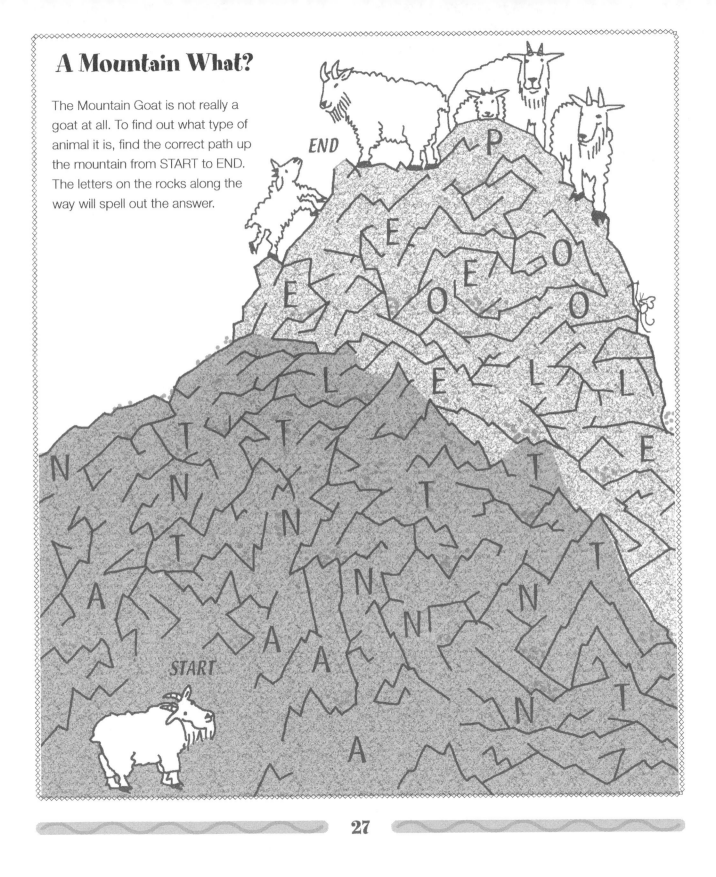

END

START

King of the Mountain

Which animal has been nicknamed "King of the Mountain"? Connect the dots from 1 to 76 to see his picture. Then, add a single straight or curved line to finish each of the letters and learn the "King's" name!

All Mixed Up

These mountain and woodland animals have gotten themselves all mixed up. Can you figure out which two animals have combined in each string of letters? **HINT:** Remove one name and the second name is left.

1. D E W O E R L F =
   <u>D E E R</u> + <u>W O L F</u>

2. R A C O P O C O O S S U N M =
   _ _ _ _ _ _ _ + _ _ _ _ _ _ _

3. B E C O A V U G E R A R =
   _ _ _ _ _ _ + _ _ _ _ _ _

4. S Q U P O R I R R C U P E L I N E =
   _ _ _ _ _ _ _ _ _ + _ _ _ _ _ _ _

5. M O O S K U S E N K =
   _ _ _ _ _ + _ _ _ _ _

Something sure is mixed up around here!

LLTAHM
AELYLA
MSALLM
PAMIAT

Lovely Llamas?

Llamas are camel-like creatures native to the Andes Mountains in South America. Their wool is soft and cuddly, and they look so cute with their long eyelashes. Can you guess what such a sweet creature does when it is angry? To find out, cross out all the L-L-A-M-A from the letter grid. Read the remaining letters left to right, and top to bottom.

mountain lion

cubs

Where's My Poult?

Look at all the animals around the edge of these two pages. Can you match each mountain or woodland mommy to their special baby? Write the names for each adult-baby pair on the lines below.

mountain goat

ADULT	BABY
_____	_____
_____	_____
_____	_____
_____	_____
_____	_____
_____	_____
_____	_____

white tailed deer

poult

beaver

pup

grizzly bear

kitten

golden eagle

What Do Skunks Have . . . ?

Fill in the letters that are not D, V, O, or P to discover the answer to the riddle.

What do skunks have that no other animals have?

fawn

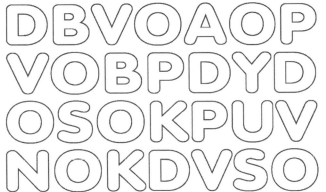

DBVOAOP
VOBPDYD
OSOKPUV
NOKDVSO

Answer: _____

kid

kit

gray wolf

wild turkey

eaglet

31

Silly Sentences

Each sentence can be completed by picking one letter of the alphabet to fill in the blanks. **HINT:** You will use six different letters!

1. __ erry __ oose __ ake __ any __ essy __ ittens.
2. __ orcupine __ arents __ aint __ rickly __ ictures.
3. __ aby __ ears __ ake __ eautiful __ rown __ read.
4. __ ive __ urry __ oxes __ ry __ resh __ rankfurters.
5. __ eary __ olves __ heel __ ooden __ heelbarrows.
6. __ idiculous __ accoons __ ead __ obot __ iddles.

EXTRA FUN: Can you say each sentence three times fast?

The Scavenger

A squirrel spends most of its life gathering food. What it doesn't eat immediately, it hides for later. First, find this squirrel's acorn stash by traveling from START to END. Then, see how many other acorns you can find hidden in the woodpile!

EXTRA FUN: How many little snails can you find sliding along the branches?

START

END

Close Cousins

Wolves live in packs of 8 to 15 family members. The group hunts together and protects its territory from other wolves. Several other wild animals are close relatives of the wolf. Solve the picture puzzles to discover the names of three other wolf kin.

1. [jacks] +L

2. C+ [eye] +O+T

3. D+ [ring] -R+O

SNAKE • RABBIT • OWL • LYNX • BEAR • BADGER • FOX • MERVIN • SHEEP • TROUT • COYOTE • MOUSE • EAGLE • WOLF • GOAT • SPIDER • JAY

V.I.M.
(Very Important Marmot)

The hoary marmot looks like a big woodchuck. It is known for making a shrill whistle that can be heard up to a mile away! However, whistling is not what makes the marmot important. Look in the word grid for the names of six animals who rely on the marmot to help them survive their harsh mountain habitat. You can choose from the names around this puzzle. First circle the names, then read the leftover letters to learn why these animals need marmots.

```
E T H E Y F
L A L L L O
G I K E C X
A T O E O N
E E A T M Y Y
R A E B O L
A R M O T T
F L O W E S
```

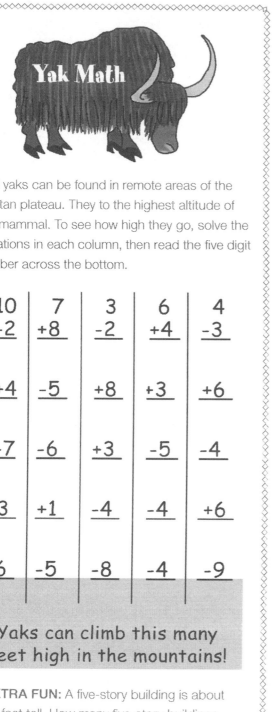

Yak Math

Wild yaks can be found in remote areas of the Tibetan plateau. They to the highest altitude of any mammal. To see how high they go, solve the equations in each column, then read the five digit number across the bottom.

10	7	3	6	4
-2	+8	-2	+4	-3
+4	-5	+8	+3	+6
-7	-6	+3	-5	-4
+3	+1	-4	-4	+6
-6	-5	-8	-4	-9

Yaks can climb this many feet high in the mountains!

EXTRA FUN: A five-story building is about 65 feet tall. How many five-story buildings equal the highest mountain a yak can climb?

Nest Numbers

A bald eagle can spread its wings over seven feet—that's bigger than the tallest teacher in your school! What's more amazing is the size of a bald eagle's nest. An eagle will reuse the same nest, adding to it every year.

Answer these questions, and add up the numbers. The total will be the number of pounds an eagle nest can weigh. Wow!

# of cards in eight decks
_____

# of keys on eight pianos
_____

# of days in two years
_____

# of dimes in $200
_____

# of pennies in six quarters
_____

It takes a big bird to make a big nest!

Here Kitty, Kitty?

A mountain lion has many names—at least 40 different ones in English and 50 more names in Spanish and Native American languages! Some names, such as cougar and puma, are familiar. Figure out the rebus puzzles to learn five other colorful names for the mountain lion!

Hide and Seek

There is the name of one mountain or woodland creature hidden in each of these sentences. Circle the ones you can find!

1. Mervin's heel kept slipping out of his shoe.

2. When the cow says "moo," see if she wants more hay.

3. At dusk, unknown insects start to buzz around.

4. Maybe Arthur is allergic to cats?

5. Let's take a stab at catching some fireflies.

6. A bad germ in the water made the campers sick.

7. A mother owl must be a very good hunter.

8. We were in awe as elephants entered the circus ring.

Mystery Marsupials

Marsupials are animals that carry their babies in a pouch (like a kangaroo). Do you know these two?

This is the only marsupial who lives in the woodlands of North America. The species has been around for 80 million years—that means they were neighbors of the dinosaurs! Connect the dots from 1 to 42 to see a picture of this "living fossil."

This marsupial lives only in the forests of east Australia. It spends most of its life sleeping and eating the leaves of its favorite tree, the eucalyptus. Connect the dots from 1 to 67 to see this shy creature. Color in the shape marked with an "N."

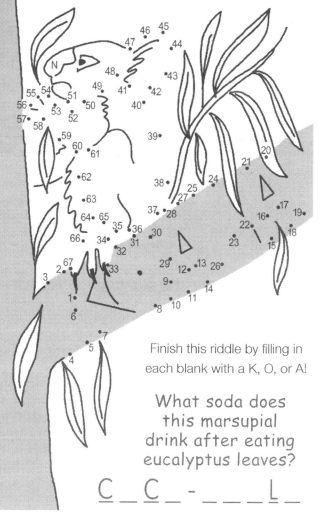

Break the code to finish the riddle, and learn the name of this mystery marsupial!

Why does the mommy

15	16	15	19	19	21	13

hate rainy days?
The kids play inside!

Finish this riddle by filling in each blank with a K, O, or A!

What soda does this marsupial drink after eating eucalyptus leaves?

C _ C _ - _ _ L

Desert Animals

Red Hot

Deserts are very hot places during the day. Fill in the blanks below using the letters R-E-D H-O-T to make six other words that describe the desert heat. **HINT:** You'll use some letters more than once!

```
L B L A Z
B A L A Z I G
L A Z A N G B L A
B L N Z B A Z A N
Z B G I L B L A A
B L A Z A I N G A
L G N I Z A L B Z
Z A G N B L L
L A G Z I
```

B U _ N I N G

F I _ _ Y

B _ _ I L I N G

S W _ L _ _ _ I N G

_ V _ N L I K _

S C _ _ _ C _ I N G

Blazing Hot

Can you stand the hot sun long enough to find the one time the word BLAZING is spelled correctly in the word grid above?

Out of the Heat

Some desert animals, like tortoises, dig a shady hole and become inactive to escape the heat. Figure out what letter is missing from each column. When the letters are filled in, read across the shaded row to learn the name for this "hot hibernation."

HINT: Each missing letter completes a familiar pattern of letters from top to bottom!

D	R	S	H	U	Z	S	H	N	M
F	T	U	J	W	B	U	J	P	O

Sssssnakes

There are many desert snakes that have similar markings. If you are looking for a particular snake—especially one that is not poisonous—you had better be careful! Find the one snake below that has these four exact markings.

- **Light stripe down back**
- **White diamond on forehead**
- **Double diamond pattern on its body that looks like this** →
- **Rattle on end of tail**

EXTRA FUN:
Can you find the one snake that has a Christmas tree on it?

Cactus Hotel

The saguaro cactus is the largest cactus in the world. It is home and food for many small animals. Unscramble the names of all the animals that rely on this saguaro.

WLO

WAHK

VODE

ZARLID

RNEW

SUMOE

ATB

PIDSER

Covered in Sand

The soil in the desert is very sandy. See if you can figure out these rebus puzzles that show four familiar words that all start with the letters S-A-N-D.

Grains of Sand

See if you can find the S-A-N-D hiding in these three sentences!

1. My aunt Sandy lives in San Diego.

2. Cassandra brought chips and dip.

3. Susan dug a hole in the sandbox.

Leaping Lizards

Desert lizards can have very different shapes: geckos are soft and squashy; whiptails have long, thin tails; skinks are little and skinny; horned lizards are covered with spikes. Can you tell which two lizards do not appear on both sides of the page?

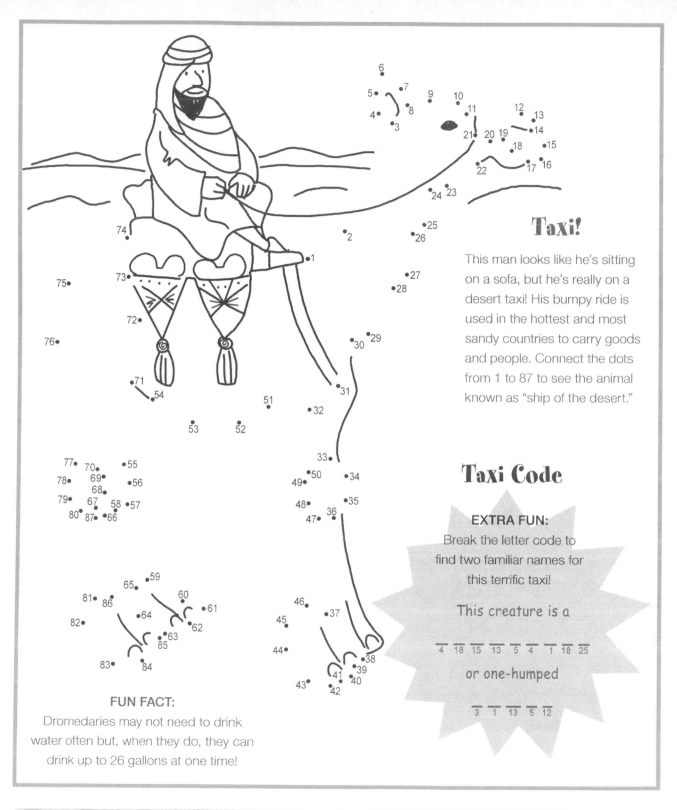

Taxi!

This man looks like he's sitting on a sofa, but he's really on a desert taxi! His bumpy ride is used in the hottest and most sandy countries to carry goods and people. Connect the dots from 1 to 87 to see the animal known as "ship of the desert."

Taxi Code

EXTRA FUN:
Break the letter code to find two familiar names for this terrific taxi!

This creature is a

$\overline{4}\ \overline{18}\ \overline{15}\ \overline{13}\ \overline{5}\ \overline{4}\ \overline{1}\ \overline{18}\ \overline{25}$

or one-humped

$\overline{3}\ \overline{1}\ \overline{13}\ \overline{5}\ \overline{12}$

FUN FACT:
Dromedaries may not need to drink water often but, when they do, they can drink up to 26 gallons at one time!

Many Meerkats

Meerkats are tough little animals that live in the Kalahari Desert of southern Africa. Desert life isn't easy, but meerkats have found a good safety system. They live in groups and work together as a team to protect each other, find food, and raise the babies. They all share the work, and they all share the benefits!

If the meerkats here gathered all the numbers hidden in this picture, then divided them equally, what number would each of them be left with?

START

Find the Oasis

An oasis is an area in the desert that always has fresh water. Many creatures rely on this precious resource. Can you help this sandgrouse find her way to the oasis? First she will have a long drink. Then she will soak her breast feathers, and bring water back to her chicks!

END

Mystery Monster

Even though monster movies and monster stories are very popular, it is difficult to find a real-life monster. One place to look is in the deserts of the southwestern United States. Complete the statements below using words from the word list. Write the one capital letter from each missing word on the line at the end of the sentence where it belongs. When you are finished, read the letters from top to bottom to discover this mystery monster's name.

Spends much of the day _____. __

Has a stubby _____ that stores fat. __

Has strong, wide _____. __

Is most _____ at night. __

Has _____ in glands in its jaw. __

Is a _____-moving creature. __

It should _____ be approached. __

Lives in _____. __

Its bite is painful, but rarely _____. __

Eats bird _____, bugs, mice, and lizards. __

Has _____ scales called beads. __

EXTRA FUN: This monster has Halloween colors! Color the sections of the drawing marked "B" black. Color the remaining sections bright orange.

Never
taIl
faTal
cLaws
Active
venoM
Round
Eggs
underGround
slOw
tunnelS

Small Survivors

The desert is home to many small creatures who seem to survive there without much difficulty. There are five of these hidden in the word puzzle below. To find them, take one letter from each column moving from left to right. Cross them off as you go—each letter can only be used once. The first creature has been done for you.

S O I T L T S
C P E U E T S
B E C D S E T
L E R C K R E
T R I M I E S

1. _SPIDERS_

2. _____

3. _____

4. _____

5. _____

Small But Deadly

This desert hunter stays sheltered during the day. At night it comes out looking for prey, which it injects with deadly venom. Fill in the blocks as directed to see this small, but dangerous creature. Would you like to meet one?

- Find box 1 and copy the pattern into square 1.
- Find box 2 and copy the pattern into square 2.
- Continue doing this until you have copied all the boxes into the grid.

Hot Days, Cool Nights

Many desert animals try to find a bit of shade during the hottest part of the day. They come out again at night to find food when it is cooler. Use this moon phase decoder to spell out a good place for shade-seekers to wait for the night.

A	B	C	D	E
F	G	H	I	J
K	L	M	N	O
P	Q	R	S	T
U	V	W	X	Y

Sand Dune Surprise

As night falls in the deserts of northern Africa and Arabia, a surprising desert creature comes out from its tunnel under the sand dunes. Fill in all the triangles (even the ones with squiggles inside) to reveal who this furry hunter is. Does he look familiar?

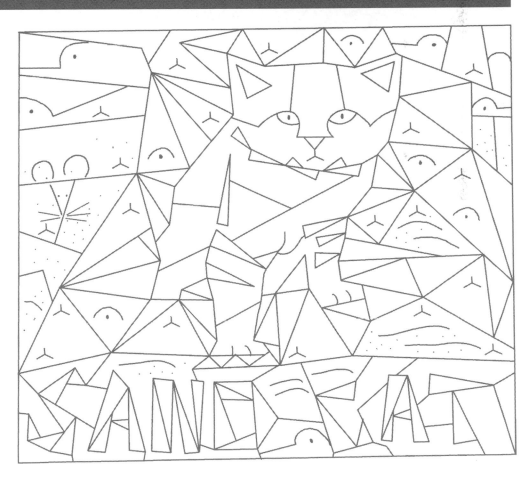

Beep Beep

The roadrunner is a desert bird known for his racing speed. Not many people know that the roadrunner is also especially good at catching rattlesnakes! See if you can find the shadow that matches the drawing of the roadrunner with his dinner.

Chapter 5

Grassland Animals

Why Did the Lion Cross the Grassland?

Find your way from START to END, collecting the letters. When you read them in order, you will discover the answer to this riddle:

Why did the lion cross the grassland?

Kangaroo Hop

There are many species of kangaroo throughout the grasslands of Australia, Tasmania, and New Guinea. Some are big and some are small, but all hop to get around. See if you can hop your way through this puzzle. All the words end in OO, just like kangaroo!

ACROSS

3. Picture etched into the skin with ink
4. Where you go to see animals from many lands
8. Masked animal you might see in your backyard
10. Pandas eat this tall and woody grass
11. What you use to wash your hair
13. What a ghost says
15. Black-and-white lake bird with a mournful cry
16. Caterpillar's home before it becomes a butterfly
17. Round house made from blocks of snow

EXTRA FUN: We've included six animals that also have OO in their names!

DOWN

1. A large monkey with a face like a dog
2. What a cow says
5. Big barnyard bird with a long neck
6. Toy musical instrument that buzzes when you hum through it
7. Sound of crying
9. Bird who pops out of a clock every hour
12. Noise of a sneeze
14. A small injury

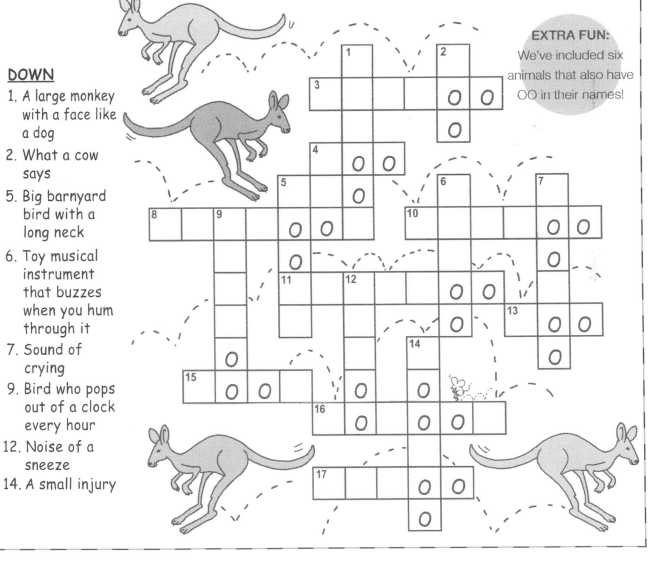

What Is It?

Use words from the list to finish this story about a very

_____ animal. Its name means "little _____

one" because it has leathery _____ around its body, a long,

scaly _____, and its face and ears are covered with

thick, _____ skin. When scared, these creatures will

jump straight _____ in the air! Originally from

_____, this "tiny tank" has moved north.

In fact, it is the state mammal of _____! Connect the dots

to see one, and solve the rebus

puzzle to learn its name.

Word List

Texas

up

armored

bands

tail

bumpy

strange

South America

A World Full of Grass

Grasslands have different names depending on where you are in the world. The five travelers below are going to visit five different grasslands. Fit the letters of each person's first name into the blank spaces of the place where they are traveling. You will to get the name of the grassland there. **HINT:** Each sentence is a rhyme!

1. Rae B. Hairy is going to the PR _ I _ I _.
   North America

2. Anna Banana is visiting the SAV _ _ _ _ _.
   Australia

3. Pete Prep will travel to the S _ _ P _ _.
   Asia & E. Europe

4. Sam and his compass look for the P _ _ PA _.
   South America

5. Pam Lampost wants to see the C _ _ _ _ OS.
   Equator

6. Lani wants rain when she goes to the P _ _ _ _ _.
   Africa

Anna

Pam

Sam

Rae

Pete

Lani

What Do You Get if You Cross a Kangaroo with an Elephant?

These two grassland animals don't live in the same place, but what if they did? Answer as many clues below as you can, and fill the letters you have into the grid. Work back and forth between the grid and clues until you discover the answer to the riddle.

	1B	2A O	3F		4E	5F	6G	
7A B	8E	9F		10D	11B	12C	13D	14D
	15C	16E	17G		18A O	19D	20G	21E
22D	23B	24G	25A T	26F	27F	28E	29C	30G

A. Tall rain shoe

$\underline{B}$ $\underline{O}$ $\underline{O}$ $\underline{T}$
7 18 2 25

B. Opposite of me

‾1‾ ‾11‾ ‾23‾

C. To be sick

‾15‾ ‾29‾ ‾12‾

D. Remove hair with razor

‾14‾ ‾10‾ ‾22‾ ‾19‾ ‾13‾

E. You barbecue on this

‾4‾ ‾21‾ ‾8‾ ‾28‾ ‾16‾

F. To fight verbally

‾27‾ ‾26‾ ‾9‾ ‾3‾ ‾5‾

G. As little as possible

‾17‾ ‾20‾ ‾30‾ ‾24‾ ‾6‾

Tallest of All

Giraffes are the tallest living animals, standing as high as 20 feet! You wouldn't think a creature this tall could easily disappear, but giraffes can! Their spots are the secret.

Fast Fact: Did you know that giraffes have blue tongues?

These brown blotches blend in with the moving shadows from the tall, thin trees found where the giraffes live. Can you find seventeen items hiding with this tall twosome? Look for: birdhouse, butterfly, star, sock, book, hammer, kite, heart, comb, question mark, mug, capital H, lamp, teapot, ghost, candle, and you know who!

Fastest of All

Using a simple number substitution (A=1, B=2, C=3 . . .) break this code to find the name of the fastest grassland animal.

$$\overline{}_{3} \ \overline{}_{8} \ \overline{}_{5} \ \overline{}_{5} \ \overline{}_{20} \ \overline{}_{1} \ \overline{}_{8}$$

EXTRA FUN: Add up all the code numbers—plus ten more—to see how many miles per hour this cat can really run!

What kind of cat should you never play cards with? A cheetah!

You Snooze, You Lose

If you move slowly in the grasslands, you will probably be caught by a predator. Can you help these antelope find the correct path through this grid using only "fast" words? You can move up and down and side to side, but not diagonally.

START

RUN	STOP	DOZE	SMILE	SWIFT
SPRINT	SPEED	SLEEP	GO	STOP
STAND	HURRY	RACE	LAZY	STROLL
DAWDLE	PAUSE	SCURRY	GALLOP	HUSTLE

END

Hide and Eat

Grasslands feed many herds of plant-eating animals (herbivores). These herds attract the meat-eating animals (carnivores) that hunt them. Look carefully to find and highlight all the herbivores and carnivores hidden in the grass.

Try using different colored markers to highlight each type—how about green for herbivores and red for carnivores?

```
G R A S S G R A S S G R A S S
R O P P I H G R A L I O N G G
A G R A S C G R A S R S G B R
S N B G R H A S S G A R A U A
S I I G Z E B R A R F A R Z S
G D S R A E G R A S F S O Z S
R W O L F T R A E S E G S A G
A G N R G A A S L G A R T R R
S R A H R H S L E O P A R D A
S A S Y A G S G P A R S I S S
G A Z E L L E R H G R A C S S
R S G N S G R A A S S R H G G
A G R A S A S G N R A S S R R
S G R A S V U L T U R E A A A
S M E R V I N G R A S S G R S
G R A S S G R A S S G R A S S
```

Herbivores:

Zebra
Gazelle
Giraffe
Bison
Hippo
Elephant
Ostrich
Mervin

Carnivores:

Cheetah
Hyena
Lion
Vulture
Buzzard
Leopard
Dingo
Wolf

Playing in the Mud

Grassland animals like the hippo, rhino, and elephant like to roll in the mud and get all dirty. Why? Each of the letters in a column belongs in one of the boxes directly below it. When you fit all the letters in the proper boxes, you will be able to read what mud does for these animals. Some letters are already done for you!

	S	T		N			N	T				H	L		
	S	R		M		O	C	A	D			A	E		
	U	U	O	T		C	R	E	E		T	E	T		
	P	K	N	N	S	E	I	E	S	I	M	I	E	I	
M	I	D	I	I	S	A	S	N	N	K	A	E	P	R
			■		■				I		A		🐭		
■	S		S			E	E		!						
		O		C				■				E	I		
	K			N					K		■				
		■	O	I		.									

HINT: Black boxes are the spaces between words.

Drew, I want you to go out and get nice and dirty today!

Aw, mom! Do I have to?

Marvelous Meadowlark

The meadowlark is one of the most common birds of the American grasslands. More than 121,000 Kansas schoolchildren voted to award this beautiful black and yellow bird a special honor. Collect the letters hidden in each section of this field. Unscramble them to see what award the meadowlark won.

__ __ __ __ __ __   __ __ __ __   __ __ __

K S A T A E R B
K A N S A S T A T E R D B I

Smooch!

A prairie dog town is a maze of tunnels that can stretch for acres across the prairie. To keep from ending up in the wrong burrow, these little critters hug and kiss each other when they meet to make sure they are from the same family.

Can you help this little dog find his way home for a smooch?

Fast Fact:
The largest prairie dog town on record was home to an estimated 35 million animals and covered 10 square miles.

END

START

The Watering Hole

Look at these six pictures. Number them in order so that the story makes sense.

Designed to Disappear

Many grassland animals have patterns on their skin to help them blend in with the grasses that surround them.

This strange creature has a different sort of pattern. Can you count the gray dots that cover his hide?

Do you think this pattern helps him to blend into the grassland?

Hop to It!

Grasshoppers can be found anyplace in the world where there are lots of leaves to eat. That's why they love the grasslands! Grasshoppers can leap about 20 times the length of their own body! Help this grasshopper hop from the bottom row of the grid to the top row by jumping only on squares that are evenly divisible by 20. You can move up, sideways, or diagonal, but only one box at a time.

50	130	80	10	90
90	30	40	110	70
110	70	10	200	50
50	90	210	230	60
210	10	80	140	130
50	160	70	30	10
10	210	20	90	50
120	40	30	110	70

START

If you were five feet tall and could jump like a grasshopper, you would land 100 feet away!

Look Fast

With legs that can stretch 11 feet in one step, an ostrich is designed for running across African grasslands! See if you can find the ten differences between these two pictures before the ostrich is gone!

## Chapter 6

Rainforest Animals

END

Going Up

The tallest trees in the rainforest stand about 130 feet tall or more. The tops of these trees get the most sunshine while only a little sunlight reaches the forest floor. Different plants and animals live at different levels in the forest. This scientist wants to study the butterflies who live at the very top of the tallest trees. Can you help her find a way up?

START

Pretty Poisonous

Poison-Dart Frogs are very small, multicolored tree frogs. Their bright colors signal predators to "stay away!" Not only will the frog taste bad, but the poisonous skin will make any animal who eats them sick. Using the color key below, color in these beautiful, but dangerous, frogs.

R = red   O = orange
B = blue   Y = yellow
G = green   P = purple
              K = black

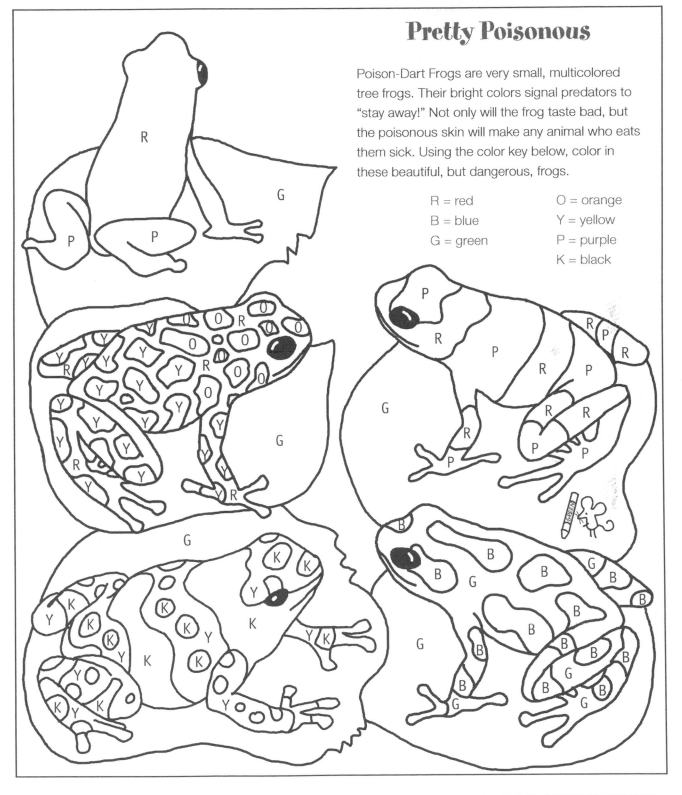

We Need Rain!

Complete the name of each rainforest animal below by adding letters from the word R-A-I-N. Then highlight these creatures where they are hiding in the letter grid. Read the leftover letters to find a rainy riddle and its answer! **HINT:** Instead of circling the names in the grid with a pencil, try using a colorful marker to highlight each name.

B _ T

_ _ T

CH _ MP _ _ ZEE

C _ OCOD _ LE

HUMM _ _ GBI _ D

_ GUA _ _

J _ GUA R

LEOP _ _ D

L _ Z _ _ D

O _ A _ GUT _ N

P _ R _ OT

S _ _ _ L

S _ _ KE

TA _ A _ TUL _

TE _ M _ TE

T _ GE _

F _ OGS

TOUC _ _

```
T O R R A P W H Y D I D
D T H I G U A N A E G O
R T O U C A N R I B A T
I L L D R A Z I L A S T
B L I C K H I S H E A D
G E E E Z N A P M I H C
N O T F R O G S H R O R
I P U G R H T H E N U O
M A M S E B R E L A T C
M R L N G A T O J T E O
U D S A I E E A I U R D
H F I I T T G H A G M I
A N T L D U S T O N I L
P P E D A R A I N A T E
I N G R E K A N S R E Y
T A R A N T U L A O E T
```

64

Big Beautiful Bills

Sometimes a tasty piece of fruit is just out of reach, or has a rind that is hard to bite. No problem! Connect the dots to see some of the most powerful beaks in the rainforest.

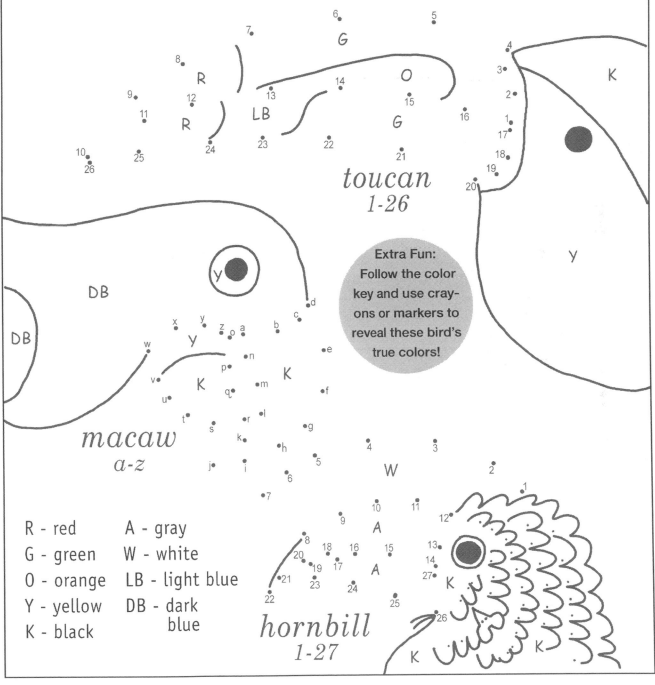

toucan
1-26

Extra Fun:
Follow the color key and use crayons or markers to reveal these bird's true colors!

macaw
a-z

R - red   A - gray
G - green   W - white
O - orange   LB - light blue
Y - yellow   DB - dark
K - black   blue

hornbill
1-27

Biiiiiig Snake

The biggest snake ever found was 28 feet long, and 44 inches around the middle. Scientists estimate that this snake weighed over 500 pounds! What is this giant's name? Place a letter in each space to make a three-letter word from left to right (we gave you a few hints). When you have done it correctly, you will find the answer spelled for you in the shaded boxes.

made of tin	C		N
before two	O		E
girl's nickname	P		T
frozen water	I		E
cat chaser	D		G
picnic insect	A		T
not even	O		D
lunch sack	B		G

Extra Fun:
If a minivan is 16 feet long, how many minivans long is this snake?

Super Bug

The rhinoceros beetle is about the size of a coffee mug. That's big for a bug! But more amazing than his size is his strength. This rainforest superstar can support 850 times his own weight! This makes it the strongest creature in the world. Stronger than an elephant? Yes—an elephant can only carry one quarter of his own weight!

Use the "Strong as a Bug" formula to figure out how many pounds you could lift if you were as strong as a rhinoceros beetle.

Strong as a Bug

of pounds you weigh:

Multiply by 850:

This is how many pounds you could lift if you were as strong as a rhinocerous beetle!

Slow as a Sloth

The sloth doesn't do anything fast. He moves so slowly that a kind of plant called algae grows on him! In the grid below are three words that also mean slow. To find them, take one letter from each column moving left to right. **HINT:** Each letter can only be used once, so cross them off as you go.

L D K E
I O Z Y
P A L Y

1._____

2._____

3._____

In Hiding

Sloths have such thick fur that they are the perfect camping place for smaller rainforest creatures. Scientists found one sloth that had three kinds of beetles, and three kinds of moths living on it! Can you find the 12 other things hiding in this sloth's fur? Look for an umbrella, candle, jumprope, paper clip, comb, feather, bowling pin, Christmas tree, fish hook, capital letter M, spatula, pencil.

Crocodile Bites

Rainforest crocodiles might be a bit smaller than their relatives in other habitats, but they are just as fierce. One of these hungry crocs has bitten into a tasty fish. But which crocodile was it? **HINT:** These crocs always swallow their dinner headfirst!

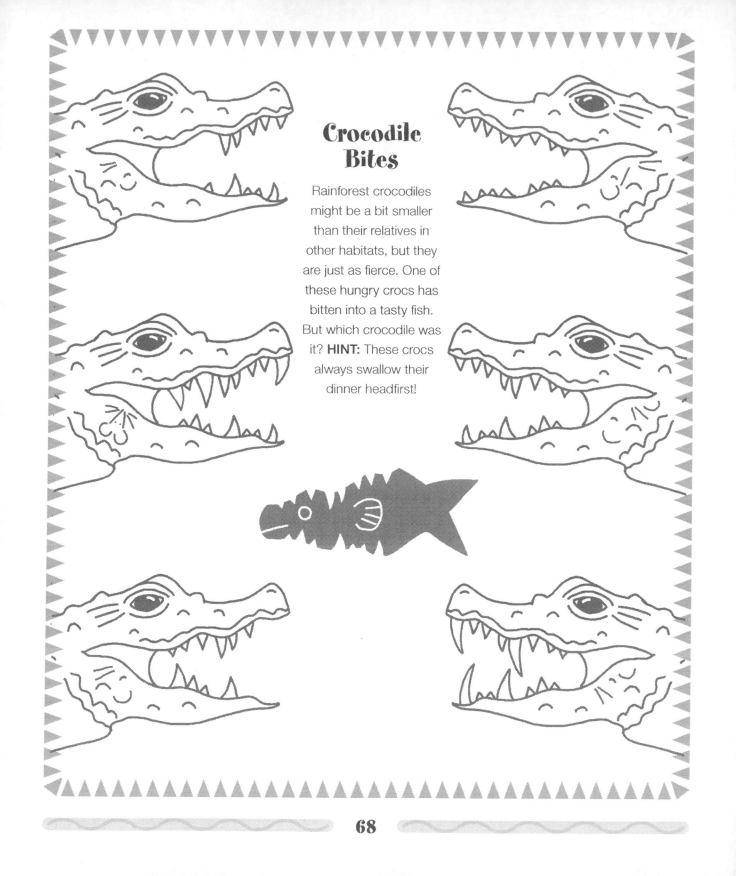

Lonely Lemur

The ring-tailed lemur is about three feet long including its tail—and more than half of that is its tail! This strange-looking primate exists in only one place in the whole world. To find out in what country his rainforests are located, follow these rules:

- Answer each clue, above.
- Fill the answers into the lemur's tail, placing one letter in each ring.
- Start from the top of the tail and work down.

R-A-I-N-F-O-R-E-S-T

Rainforests are home to about half the world's animal species! Just as there are a huge variety of animals living in the rainforests, there are many, many words "living" in the letters R-A-I-N-F-O-R-E-S-T. Bet you can find at least fifty!

Who Am I?

Find the capital letter in each clue below that does not start the sentence. Unscramble the six letters to find the name of this mysterious rainforest cat.

I am the largest cat in the Americas.

I am a solitaRy animal.

I have powerful Jaws.

I swim And climb very well.

I like to ambUsh my prey.

I snarl and Growl.

Tiny Farmers

Leafcutter ants are smart—they grow their own food! They take snips of rainforest plants to their nest. After chewing the plants, they spit them out and use the mush to grow a tasty fungus. How many leafcutter ants do you see here? If these ants form eight columns, how many ants will be in each row?

EXTRA FUN: Which ant is going the wrong way? Which four ants aren't carrying leaves? Which ant isn't carrying anything?

Breezy Butterflies

Believe it or not, there isn't much wind in a rainforest! Most rainforest plants need the animals and insects who live there to move their pollen and seeds around. Butterflies flit from flower to flower drinking nectar, and carry pollen from one plant to another as they go.

Draw the second half of this butterfly to match the half shown. Use the grid lines to guide you.

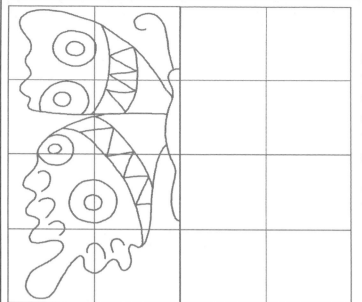

Batty for Fruit

Fruit bats use their keen sense of smell to find ripe rainforest fruit. By spitting out the seeds or dropping them as they fly through the forest, bats help new fruit trees to grow. Choose one of the dropped letters to add to each fruit. Then unscramble the letters and write the correct fruit names on the dotted lines.

1. _ _ _

2. _ _ _ _ _

3. _ _ _ _ _ _

Barrel of Monkeys?

The rainforest is home to monkeys and apes. People tend to get these two mixed up, but they are actually two different kinds of animals. However, when it comes to a good joke, apes and monkeys both enjoy a good laugh!

Collect all the words of the same number. Write them in the correct order on the numbered lines to get the answers.

3 B	5 hot	4 During	2 Jungle
4 showers	6 Chocolate	1 Chimpan	5 baboon
2 Bells	1 Sea	3 Ape	4 -ril
4 Ape	3 C's	5 air	6 chimp

1. Where's a good place for monkeys to swim?
   In the _____

2. What's a monkey's favorite Christmas carol?

   _____

3. What does a monkey learn in kindergarten?
   His _____

4. When do monkeys fall from the sky?

   _____

5. What kind of monkey can fly?
   A _____

6. What's a monkey's favorite cookie?

   _____

## Chapter 7

Farm Animals

Above the Barn

Most people think of large animals like cows and horses when they think of the creatures that live in a barn. But if you look up at big barns, you will often see the darting shapes of tiny barn swallows flitting in and out. Many barns have small, round holes built into them especially for the swallows to use. Why do farmers like to have these little birds around?

Break the letter-shifting code by writing the letters either one before or one after the letters shown. Then color every square with a dot in the middle. **HINT:** You can write your answer over the code letters with a dark crayon or marker.

UIFZ FBU MPUT
BOE MPUT PG

In the Barn

Amazingly, there are a small number of barns in this country that are more than 300 years old! These buildings were as important to farmers then as they still are today—as a safe home for farm animals.

Can you tell the names of the animals that live in this barn by the few letters showing through the windows?

ONK
CO URK GOA
ICK ⊠ORS HEE
⊠
OOS

START

Cat and Mouse

If there is a barn full of grain, it is certain that there is a barn full of mice. That's why most farmers think it's a good idea to have a cat or two who live in the barn. In fact, more than 4,000 years ago, the farmers in Egypt first discovered how helpful it was to have a cat around to protect their harvest! See who makes it to the pile of grain first—cat or mouse. After you find the correct paths through the maze, go back and count each corner turned as one point. The critter with the fewest points wins!

END

START

Moo Tunes

Dairy cows can produce up to six gallons of milk a day. Some people believe that if a cow listens to music that she likes while being milked, she gives more milk! Using the key at the bottom of the page, figure out which cow is listening to her favorite tunes and has produced the most cups of milk.

EXTRA FUN: Can you figure out which cow is in love? Thinking of dessert? Really happy?

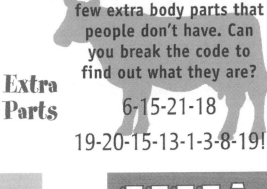

Extra Parts

A cow seems to have a few extra body parts that people don't have. Can you break the code to find out what they are?

6-15-21-18

19-20-15-13-1-3-8-19!

1 gallon = 2 half gallons = 4 quarts = 8 pints = 16 cups

Pig Pen

On a hot day, a poor pig can't sweat to cool off like you do. Pigs have no sweat glands! That's why pigs love to roll in nice, squishy mud. It not only cools them off, but helps protect their tender skin from the sun. Can you find the ten differences between these two pig pens?

Trick Question 1

Can you spell PIG using nine letters? Sure you can! Use a simple number substitution (A=1, B=2, C=3 . . .) to see how it is done.

Trick Question 2

All of Farmer Jane's pigs are brown except one, and all of her pigs are pink except one. How many brown and pink pigs does Farmer Jane have?

Move Along!

Farmers all over the world rely on dogs to help move their flocks of sheep from one place to another. These dogs learn to obey specific voice or whistle commands. Sometimes the dogs have to be extra clever at their work, like running across the backs of tightly packed sheep! Use these directions to help the dog separate the sheep by color and get them into the proper pens.

Cross out the following kinds of words:

- Four-letter words that rhyme with SHEEP
- Colors spelled with six letters
- Two-letter words with A
- Words that start with GRE

Walk up!

AN
NO
KEEP
GRAY
GREEN
OR
WHITE
CHERRY
SHEEP
HERE

AX
GREAT
GRAY
PURPLE
SHEEP
GREET
SEEP
HERE
AM
SHEEP
HERE

GREED
HEAP

LEAP
WHITE
AS
MAROON
SHEEP
YELLOW
ONLY
AT

Old MacDonald Had a Farm . . .

If you know the next line of this familiar song, you'll know which letters are missing from the names of the farm animals below. Fill them in! HINT: We took the As and the Us, too.

Next, fill in the numbered grid with the sound each animal makes. This time we left you a few E-I-E-I-Os to help!

Across
1. G _ _ _ S _
2. C _ T
6. R _ _ ST _ R
9. D _ C K
10. H _ R S _
13. S H _ _ P

Down
1. D _ N K _ Y
3. C _ W
4. C H _ C K _ N
5. D _ G
7. P _ G
8. M _ _ S _
11. T _ R K _ Y
12. G _ _ T

Lawn Mowers

Old MacDonald wants to move his sheep from the barn to the roadside to eat the weeds that grow there. Travel one space at a time making compound words as you go. You can move up and down, and side to side—but not diagonally.

START

BARN	YARD	STICK	SOME	BODY	BUILD
HOME	WORK	SHOP	HAND	GUARD	ONE
WORK	OUT	LIFT	OFF	RAIL	HEAD
BOOK	SIDE	HOME	BEAT	ROAD	SIDE

END

Chicken Scratch

Did you know that not all chickens are white with a red comb? Some have spots, and some have stripes. Some have crazy feathers that make it look as if they are wearing a dust mop on their head! There are more than 350 different combinations of chicken "styles." See if you can answer the following questions:

- How many different kinds of chickens do you see here?
- Are there more striped or solid dark chickens?
- There is only one of which kind of chicken?

Nobody Here But Us Chickens

This chicken coop is full of letters that will make OO words.
Can you figure them out using the clues below?

1. An owl makes this sound, not a chicken = _ 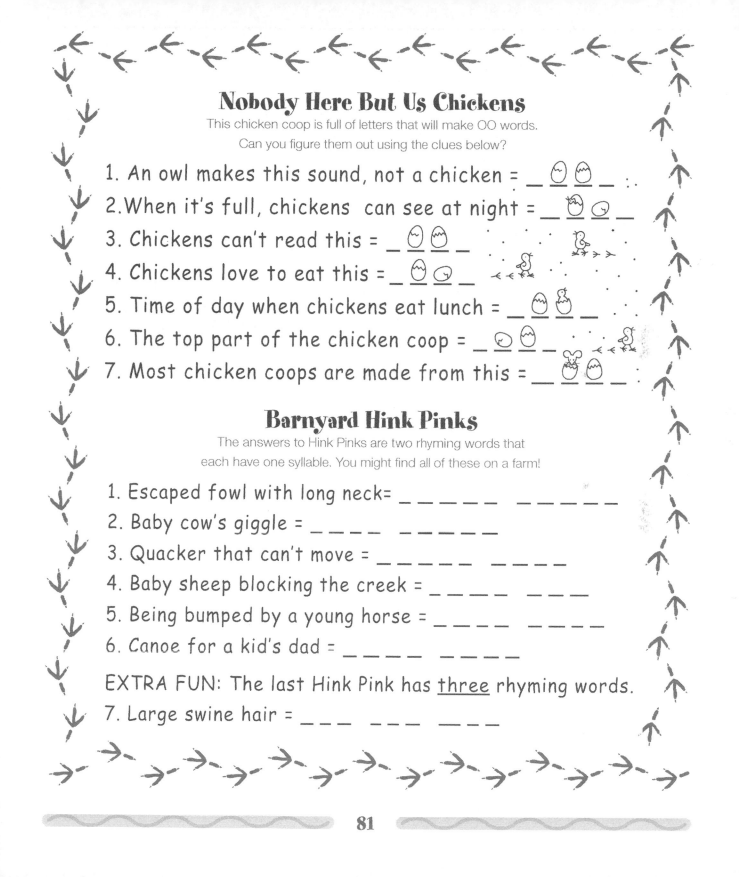 _ _ .
2. When it's full, chickens can see at night = _ _ _ _
3. Chickens can't read this = _ _ _ _
4. Chickens love to eat this = _ _ _ _
5. Time of day when chickens eat lunch = _ _ _ _
6. The top part of the chicken coop = _ _ _ _
7. Most chicken coops are made from this = _ _ _ _

Barnyard Hink Pinks

The answers to Hink Pinks are two rhyming words that
each have one syllable. You might find all of these on a farm!

1. Escaped fowl with long neck= _ _ _ _ _ _   _ _ _ _ _ _
2. Baby cow's giggle = _ _ _ _ _   _ _ _ _ _
3. Quacker that can't move = _ _ _ _ _ _   _ _ _ _ _
4. Baby sheep blocking the creek = _ _ _ _ _   _ _ _ _ _
5. Being bumped by a young horse = _ _ _ _ _   _ _ _ _
6. Canoe for a kid's dad = _ _ _ _   _ _ _ _

EXTRA FUN: The last Hink Pink has <u>three</u> rhyming words.

7. Large swine hair = _ _ _   _ _ _   _ _ _

If the Shoe Fits

A horse's hoof is like a giant toenail! And like a toenail, hoofs can break and crack. A horseshoe is a U-shaped plate that is nailed on the bottom of a horse's hoof to protect it. Figure out where to put each of the scrambled letters. They all fit under their own columns. When you have filled in the grid correctly, you will know why some people have a horseshoe even though they do not have a horse! **HINT:** We left you one horseshoe for luck.

Where do sick ponies go to get better?

The horsepital!

What Kind of Allergy . . .

What kind of allergy makes a horse sneeze?

Color in all the shapes that have the letters A-C-H-O-O to find out!

ACHOO

Funny Farm

Not all farmers raise the usual cows, pigs, or chickens. Some farmers choose animals that are a little more unusual! Connect the dots to find a picture of one animal that many people now raise on their farms. Do you know what country has this creature as a symbol of their nation?

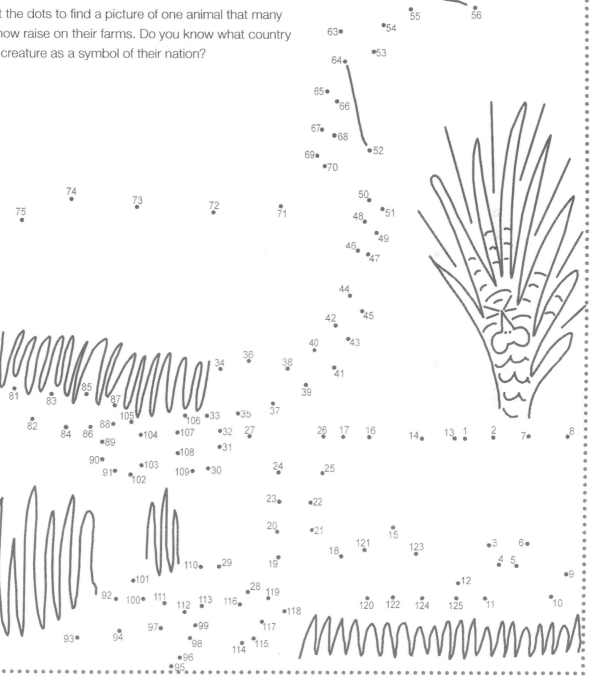

Where Is Everybody?

Cow convinced all the animals to go somewhere. Crack the track code to find out where they went.

H T M V E W N I S O

## Chapter 8

Pets

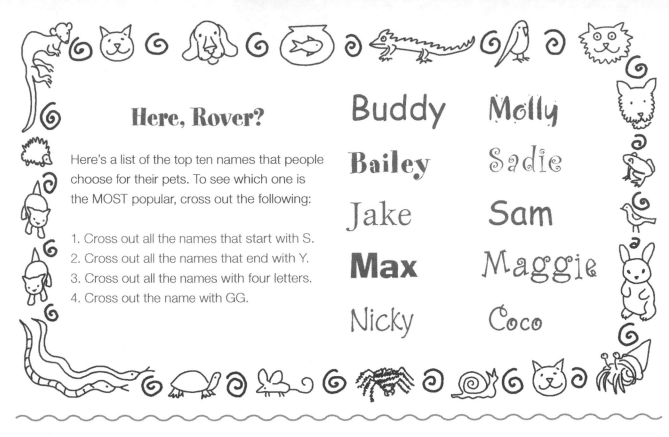

Here, Rover?

Here's a list of the top ten names that people choose for their pets. To see which one is the MOST popular, cross out the following:

1. Cross out all the names that start with S.
2. Cross out all the names that end with Y.
3. Cross out all the names with four letters.
4. Cross out the name with GG.

Buddy   Molly

Bailey   Sadie

Jake   Sam

Max   Maggie

Nicky   Coco

Hungry Herd

Who will be the first pet to get breakfast? See if you can figure it out from the clues provided.

Ramona eats after Rosie.
Rosie eats before Stormy, but after Neudge.

Harry and Rosie eat together.
Stormy always eats last.

Stormy   Rosie   Ramona   Harry   Neudge

Perfect Parakeet

There are many parakeets in this cage, but Andrew wants one in particular. Find the bird that has all the following:

- white body
- dark wing
- long tail
- 3 spots near beak
- 3 stripes on forehead

Sounds Like . . .

How many pet sounds can you make from the letters listed below? Letters can be used more than once, but notice that not all the letters in the alphabet are available to you. Even so, we bet you can make at least ten noisy words.

**A B E G H I K L M
O P Q U R S T W Y**

1. _____
2. _____
3. _____
4. _____
5. _____
6. _____
7. _____
8. _____
9. _____
10. _____

Kate's Kittens

Which of these shadows exactly matches Kate's kittens playing with their new toys?

CAT NIP

Pets on the Run

Some pets are tricky and sneak off when you're not looking! See if you can put all these pet words back where they belong. Choose from the word parts around the page. Combine two, three, or even four parts to make complete words that answer the clues below. Each finished word will have a P-E-T at either the beginning or the end!

CAR   EUM   PET   PET   UN   A

FY

PET

IA

PET   PUP   AL

PET

A rug = _ _ _ _ _ _

Small = _ _ _ _ _ _

Part of a flower = _ _ _ _ _ _

Hand toy = _ _ _ _ _ _ _

Fancy slip = _ _ _ _ _ _ _ _ _ _

Gasoline = _ _ _ _ _ _ _ _ _ _ _

Castle wall = _ _ _ _ _ _ _ _

Musical instrument = _ _ _ _ _ _ _ _

Turn into stone = _ _ _ _ _ _ _ _

Summer flower = _ _ _ _ _ _ _ _

PAR   COAT

TI

PET

ITE   TRUM   PET   ROL   RI   PET

I Love My Pet

Ask a friend or someone in your family to help you finish this story. Don't show them the story first! Ask your helper for the kind of word needed for each blank line (a description is written underneath). Write in the words your helper gives you, then read the story out loud.

I have a very _____ pet named _____.
                     descriptive word   *funny name*

He is _____ feet tall and weighs _____ pounds. He is a beautiful
       number   *number*

shade of _____, with _____ _____
         color   *different color*   *pattern (stripes, etc.)*

on his _____. I keep him in a _____
          body part   *container*

in the _____. _____ loves
       place in the house   *same name used on line one*

to eat _____! I need to _____
          food   *action word*

him around the block _____ times a day. I love my pet!
                        number

The Dog Walker

Can you tell which leash goes to which pet?

1.
2.
3.

Furry Friends

Are there more white or gray mice?

Are there more mice or gerbils?

Do all the guinea pigs and rabbits have the same pattern?

There is only one of which pet?

guinea pig

gerbil

mouse

hamster

rabbit

Silly Sentences

Each sentence can be completed by picking one letter of the alphabet to fill in the blanks. Can you say each sentence three times fast?

1. __ arry's __airy __amster __id __amburgers.

2. __enny's __retty __arrot __erched __erpendicular.

3. __red's __inest __ishes __ixed __ive __ences.

4. __avid's __irty __og __rew __ancing __inosaurs.

5. __ara's __razy __at __ooked __old __ucumbers.

6. __imon's __even __nakes __ipped __weet __odas.

7. __sabel's __tchy __guana __gnored __nsects.

Pet Hair Is Everywhere

No home with furry pets is complete without it! Finish the names of these familiar pieces of clothing and furniture by adding the letters from P-E-T H-A-I-R.

SOF__   S__O____S

C_____   J__CK____

D____SS   T-S_____

SU____   SW_____

____N__S   B__DS____D

92

What Pet Did Annie Get?

Annie just came home with her new pet. Can you figure out what it is? Cross off the pets Annie didn't get as you read these statements. When you're finished, only one pet will be left!

Does not live underwater.
Does not have wings.
Does not have a shell.

Does not have fur.
Does not have eight legs.
Does not have spots.

Too Close!

James has taken pictures of all his friend's pets. Unfortunately, he zoomed in too close. Can you tell what kind of animals these are?

1. _____
2. _____
3. _____
4. _____
5. _____
6. _____
7. _____
8. _____
9. _____

Funny Fish

Use the clues to fill in the spaces in all of the fish. The last letter of one answer is the first letter of the next answer. When you are done, place the numbered letters on the lines to answer the riddle!

1 Kind of lizard
2. Hooting bird
3. Not quiet
4. Can't hear
5. Short Friday
6. Creative thoughts
7. Opposite of North

What are the most expensive fish at the pet store?

___ ___ ___ ___ ___ ___ ___ ___
1.   2.   3.   4.   5.   6.   7.   8.

First Fish

Sam has taken a lot of care to make sure the aquarium is just right for his new fish, Ruby. Can you find everything he had to get to keep her happy and well? Search for the aquarium supplies in the word grid. Use a YELLOW marker or crayon to color the squares containing the letters of each word.

EXTRA FUN: Color in the boxes according to the color key to get a picture of Ruby!

Y = YELLOW   X = DARK BLUE
Z = SAND   B = LIGHT BLUE
G = GREEN

SUPPLIES:

HEATER

COVER

PUMP

GRAVEL

FISH FOOD

FILTER

ROCKS

PLANTS

A	O	J	D	J	C	D	C	I	A	I	D	C	A	O	H	O	I	A
C	F	A	J	C	W	O	W	A	K	O	I	D	J	I	B	C	J	I
D	W	D	H	J	D	A	K	Y	Y	Y	A	K	A	F	I	J	B	W
A	I	J	O	A	H	I	I	J	Y	Y	Y	J	W	C	K	W	H	A
W	K	Y	Y	C	C	H	Y	S	T	N	A	L	P	H	J	B	C	F
A	J	Y	Y	Y	F	H	E	A	T	E	R	Y	U	Y	O	D	F	G
H	C	I	F	I	L	T	E	R	Y	R	Y	X	M	Y	L	F	D	G
D	A	O	I	F	I	S	H	F	O	O	D	Y	P	E	Y	A	H	G
G	F	H	Y	Y	O	R	E	V	O	C	Y	Y	V	Y	O	I	O	G
G	H	Y	Y	Y	J	O	Y	Y	Y	K	Y	A	Y	C	H	G	J	G
G	I	Y	Y	I	G	D	I	W	Y	S	R	W	A	I	C	G	D	G
G	O	H	C	F	G	W	A	O	A	G	J	D	H	I	F	G	H	G
G	A	W	J	C	G	J	D	I	H	F	C	C	I	O	W	G	I	G
Z	Z	Z	Z	Z	Z	Z	Z	Z	Z	Z	Z	Z	Z	Z	Z	Z	Z	Z

Listen to Your Pet!

See if you can tell what each pet needs to stay healthy and safe by listening to what they say. Write the answers in the grid. We did one for you!

ACROSS
4 "Dinner time!"
5 "I've had enough playing today!"
7 "Let's go for a walk!"
9 "I'm covered with mud and gunk!"

DOWN
1 "Don't let the cat eat me!"
2 "I sure am thirsty!"
3 "Let's have some fun!"
6 "I don't feel so good!"
8 "Where can I find you?"

How do you keep a dog from barking in the front yard?

PBARKUBARKTBARK
HBARKIBARKMBARK
IBARKNBARK
TBARKHBARKEBARK
BBARKABARKCBARKKBARK
YBARKABARKRBARKDBARK!

Dog Talk

Figure out the secret dog language and you'll know the answer to this riddle.

96

Chapter 9

Endangered Species

Once Upon a Time . . .

NOW

Many species of animals that used to live on Earth don't exist here anymore. Work backwards through the maze from the crocodile (NOW) to its ancient relative, the Deinosuchus (THEN).

E
E
X
E
X
T
C
T
T
X
E
I T
N
N
I
N
C
I
N
N
C
N
C C
THEN
C
E
T
E
T

Collect letters along the path to spell a word that describes species that no longer exist.

We Love Dinosaurs!

Although they have been extinct for more than 65 million years, we still find dinosaurs fascinating. Can you fit these seven dinosaurs into the crisscross? We've left you some D-I-N-O-S to get you started

VELOCIRAPTOR

STEGOSAURUS

APATOSAURUS

IGUANODON

ALLOSAURUS

TRICERATOPS

T. REX

Animals from the Past

Fossils are the remains of an animal's body that have been turned into stone over time. They show us how ancient animals looked. Some fossils are so delicate that you can see an insect's wing. Some fossils are so huge they need to be moved with a truck!

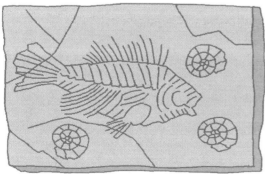

Can you find the six differences between these two fossils?

Going Backward

Extinction didn't only happen to dinosaurs. Extinction is still going on today! All animals, including humans, need room to grow and food to eat. If two groups want to live in the same place or eat the same food, one group might get pushed right off the planet! Use a simple substitution code (A=1, B=2, C=3, etc.) to discover two things that can cause a modern animal to become extinct.

8-1-2-9-20-1-20   4-5-19-20-18-21-3-20-9-15-14

_____   _____

16 - 15 - 12 - 12 - 21 - 20 - 9 - 15 - 14

_____

Moving Forward

While there are forces that work against animals causing them to become endangered or extinct, there are forces working to help protect animals, too! Use a reverse substitution code (A=Z, B=Y, C=X, etc.) to discover two things that can help endangered animals!

K O Z M G R M T   G I V V H

_____   _____

M Z G R L M Z O   K Z I P H

_____   _____

Butterfly Blues

Caterpillars of the Karner Blue butterfly like to eat just one thing—leaves of the wild blue lupine. Unfortunately, a lot of wild lupine grows where people want to put buildings! Luckily, this caterpillar has found a little patch of lupine left. Cross out the leaves that have letters that appear two or more times. How many leaves are left to eat?

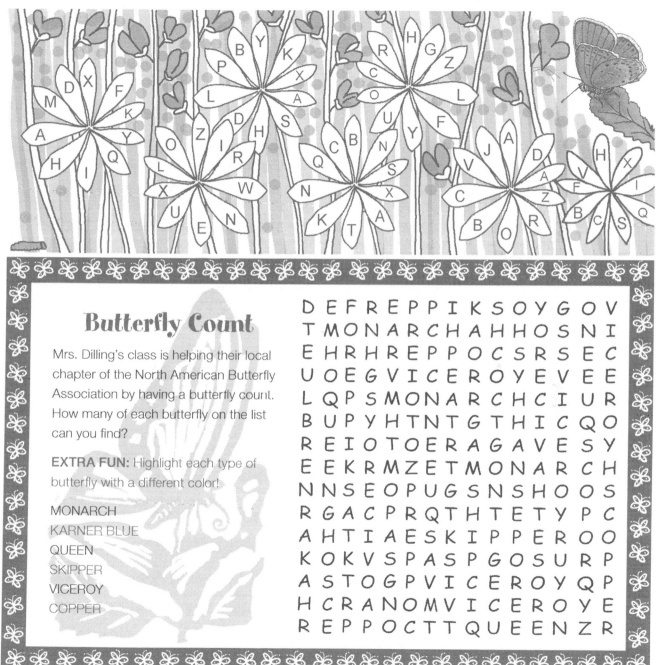

Butterfly Count

Mrs. Dilling's class is helping their local chapter of the North American Butterfly Association by having a butterfly count. How many of each butterfly on the list can you find?

EXTRA FUN: Highlight each type of butterfly with a different color!

MONARCH
KARNER BLUE
QUEEN
SKIPPER
VICEROY
COPPER

```
D E F R E P P I K S O Y G O V
T M O N A R C H A H H O S N I
E H R H R E P P O C S R S E C
U O E G V I C E R O Y E V E E
L Q P S M O N A R C H C I U R
B U P Y H T N T G T H I C Q O
R E I O T O E R A G A V E S Y
E E K R M Z E T M O N A R C H
N N S E O P U G S N S H O O S
R G A C P R Q T H T E T Y P C
A H T I A E S K I P P E R O O
K O K V S P A S P G O S U R P
A S T O G P V I C E R O Y Q P
H C R A N O M V I C E R O Y E
R E P P O C T T Q U E E N Z R
```

Gentle Giants

There are only two marine mammals that feed exclusively on vegetation, eating more than 30 pounds of plants in one day! Answer the clues on each creature to learn its name.

Because they swim slowly and near the surface, these creatures often get hit by boats! Help these two have a safe swim by fixing this sign. Use only straight lines!

BOATS, GO SLOW! WATCH FOR ANIMALS!

grown-up boy · first letter · golf ball stand

past tense of dig · reverse of no · letter before H

EXTRA FUN: These two types of animals look very similar. Can you see one big difference between the two?

Save the Tiger!

Tigers are solitary animals that need a lot of space to call their own. Some Asian countries are giving land back to the tigers and stocking it with prey to give these animals a chance to survive. Follow the directions below to fill in the signs. These could be posted all around the tiger's new home! HINT: Use an orange marker to fill in the squares.

1. Fill in all the blocks across the tops of each sign except for 14.
2. Fill in all the blocks across the bottom of signs 2, 3, 4, 7, 10, and 12.
3. Fill in all the blocks on the left side of signs 3, 4, 5, 7, 8, 9, 12, and 13.
4. Fill in all the blocks on the right side of sign 12.
5. Fill in all the blocks down the middle of signs 1, 2, 6, 10, and 11.
6. Fill in all the blocks across the middle of signs 4, 7, and 14.
7. Fill in just the center block of signs 5, 8, 9, and 13.
8. Fill in the boxes with dots of signs 3, 5, 8, 9, 13, and 14.

103

Poor Rhino

High prices are paid for the horns of rhinoceroses. Why would anyone want them? To find out, answer each question below and put the letters into their proper place in the grid. Work back and forth until you have the answer.

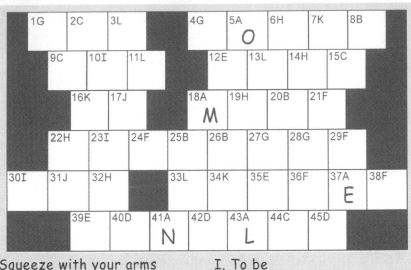

1G	2C	3L		4G	5A O	6H	7K	8B
9C	10I	11L		12E	13L	14H	15C	
16K	17J		18A M	19H	20B	21F	
22H	23I	24F	25B	26B	27G	28G	29F
30I	31J	32H		33L	34K	35E	36F	37A E	38F
	39E	40D	41A N	42D	43A L	44C	45D	

A. Sour fruit
 L   E   M   O   N
 43 37 18   5 41

B. To be ill
 ___ ___ ___ ___
  8 25 26 20

C. Body part under a hat
 ___ ___ ___ ___
  2 44   9 15

D. Unhappy
 ___ ___ ___
 45 40 42

E. Squeeze with your arms
 ___ ___ ___
 39 12 35

F. Selfish desire for more
 ___ ___ ___ ___ ___
 36 38 21 29 24

G. Skinny
 ___ ___ ___ ___
  1   4 27 28

H. Picture in your sleep
 ___ ___ ___ ___ ___
 32   6 14 19 22

I. To be
 ___ ___ ___
 30 10 23

J. Opposite of yes
 ___ ___
 31 17

K. Light brown color
 ___ ___ ___
 16 34   7

L. What a plant grows from
 ___ ___ ___ ___
 13   3 11 33

Gotcha!

How did the clever park ranger protect the rhino from being hunted for his horn?

Replace the missing vowels and connect the dots to find out!

H_ g_v_
th_ rh_no
_ b_ll
_nst__d!

104

Island Attraction

The Galapagos tortoise, which can weigh more than 500 pounds apiece, were once hunted for their meat and oil. Now they are protected by law. Follow the directions in this tortoise's shell. When you are done, you will know which humans, and their vacation dollars, have become very helpful in protecting these turtles!

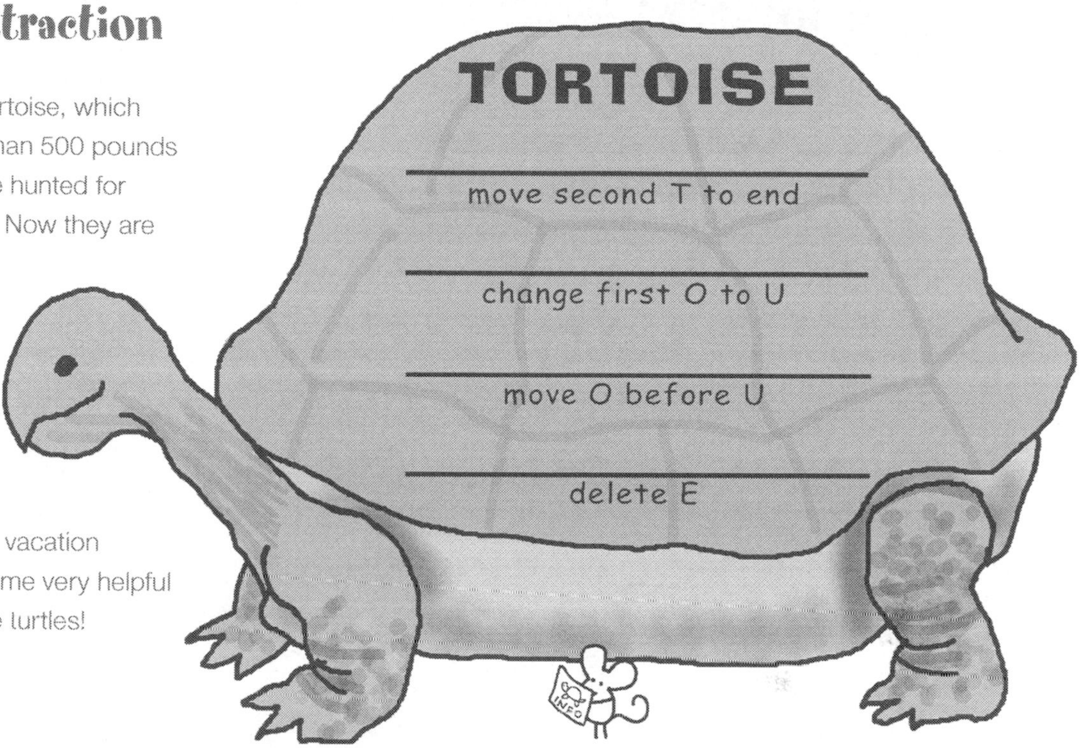

TORTOISE

___

move second T to end

___

change first O to U

___

move O before U

___

delete E

Say Cheese!

There is a new kind of hunter who doesn't need to kill an animal to take it home. This kind of hunter is much more interested in keeping animals alive and well. Use the decoder to find out what this hunter uses instead of a gun.

◆ ● ■ ▲ ▼ ★
A C E L M R

There's No Place Like Home

Mountain gorillas are gentle, giant apes that live in Central Africa. Unfortunately, much of their forest is being cleared for farmland. People who care about the gorillas are working hard to keep enough land as good gorilla habitat. You can help by crossing out all the harmful words in this grid. Circle the synonyms for PROTECT!

defend   neglect   destroy
secure   SUPPORT   care for
FAIL   guard   *ruin*   harm
ignore   burn   SHIELD
preserve   uproot   save
damage   shelter   rescue
watch over   HELP   *pollute*

Sad Panda/ Glad Panda

More and more people are trying to save endangered animals. You can help Sad Panda move through the maze so he is Happy Panda at the end! Make a path that alternates sad and glad. You can move up and down, or side-to-side, but not diagonally. If you hit a Mad Panda, you are going in the wrong direction!

START

END

106

What Can I Do?

Heather doesn't like to read about so many endangered animals. She decided to write a letter to her friend, Keith. Unfortunately, Heather's typing is not very good. Look at the keyboard, below. Can you figure out what went wrong—and what Heather was trying to say?

E 3 Q 4   I 3 8 5 Y ,

8   2 9 7 0 E   0 8 I 3   5 9

Y 3 0 *   Q H 8 J Q 0 W .

8   I H 9 2   5 Y Q 5

8 W   6 9 7 4   U 9 G .

★ 0 3 Q W 3

5 3 0 0   J 3   J 9 4 3 !

Y 3 Q 5 Y 3 4

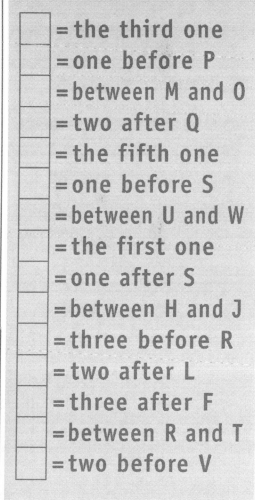

Keyboard rows:

`1 2 3 4 5 6 7 8 9 *`

`Tab  Q W E R T Y U I O P`

`Caps  A S D F G H J K L :`

`Shift  Z X C V B N M , . ?`

`Ctrl  Alt          Alt`

Be Like Me!

Here is Keith's answer:

Dear Heather,
I protect the Earth's natural resources, including the animals. My job has a really long name. To find out what it is, crack the code and fill the correct letters into the boxes. Read the letters from top to bottom. You can be one too!

☐	= the third one
☐	= one before P
☐	= between M and O
☐	= two after Q
☐	= the fifth one
☐	= one before S
☐	= between U and W
☐	= the first one
☐	= one after S
☐	= between H and J
☐	= three before R
☐	= two after L
☐	= three after F
☐	= between R and T
☐	= two before V

Home to Us All

Color in all the shapes that have the letters E-A-R-T-H for an important message!

Appendix 1: Resources

There is a vast amount of information on animals available in books and on Web sites. Below we have listed a few of our favorites.

Books

Weird Friends: Unlikely Allies in the Animal Kingdom
By Jose Aruego & Ariane Dewey (2002)
A fun and fascinating book about real animal companions who work together to make life in the wild a little better and safer for each other.

Zoo-ology
By Joelle Jolivet (2003)
Giant-sized pages full of eye-catching animals and interesting facts. This book seems to have all the animals in the world, many divided into fun categories such as "Black and White," "Underground," and "Up at Night."

What Do You Do With a Tail Like This?
By Steve Jenkins & Robin Page (2003)
A beautifully illustrated question and answer book.

Actual Size
By Steve Jenkins (2004)
How long is an anteater's tongue, really? How big is your hand compared to that of a mountain gorilla? Animals, large and small, are impressively pictured at their actual size.

Tooth and Claw
By Ted Lewin (2003)
Fourteen of the author's real-life experiences with wild animals.

DK Guide to Mammals
By Ben Morgan (2003)
Packed with interesting information and breathtaking photographs.

There's a Frog in My Throat: 440 Animal Sayings a Little Bird Told Me
By Loreen Leedy & Pat Street (2003)
An imaginative and amusing compilation of all the animal sayings you have ever heard, and then some. See you later, alligator!

Web Sites

www.worldwildlife.org
Log in here for the latest news about endangered species. Take quizzes, play games—even send wildlife postcards to your friends.

www.kidsplanet.org
This is one of the American Library Association's "Great Web Sites." It is very child friendly and is chock full of interactive stories, games, and puzzles.

www.amnh.org
The American Museum of Natural History has created a multi-award–winning Web site packed with fun and fascinating information and great "stuff to do."

Appendix 2: Now Where Did I See That . . . ?

See if you can find each of these nine animal picture pieces somewhere in this book. Are you ready? There are almost one hundred pages of puzzles to look through! Write the name of the puzzle each piece is from in the space under each box. **HINT:** There is only one picture piece from each chapter.

1.

2.

3.

4.

5.

6.

7.

8.

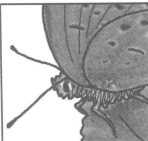

9.

page v • Introduction Word Search

The leftover letters read: There are over four thousand species of mammals!

page 2 • Cold Creatures Criss-Cross

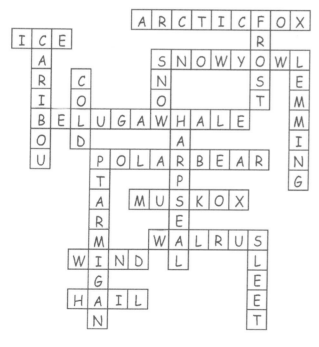

page 3 • Where Are We?

Answer: Lost! No penguins live in the arctic. Most of them live in Antarctica!

page 4 • White in Winter

C	A	M	O	U	F	L	A	G	E
E-2	first	N-1	L+3	T+1	sixth	O-3	first	H-1	D+1

page 4 • Where's the Fox?

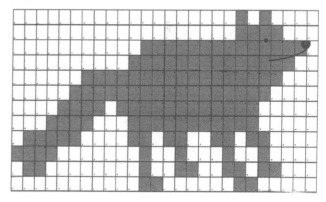

page 5 • Polar Bear Treats

1. MALONS = (S) A L M O N
2. SRIBEER = B E R R I (E) S
3. RALSWU = W (A) L R U S
4. MIGNELMS = (L) E M M I N G S
5. GESG = E G G (S)

PUZZLE ANSWERS

page 5 • Totally Cool

1. CHILLY
2. FRIGID
3. FROZEN
4. WINTRY
5. FROSTY

page 6 • What's a "Whale-Horse"?

page 7 • Common Cold

1D	2E	3G	4E		5A	6D	7F	8G		9B	10A	11C	12C
T	H	E	Y		B	O	T	H		H	A	V	E

13F	14G	15H	16H	17D	18E		19C	20A	21B	22G	23C	
H	O	L	L	O	W		H	A	I	R	S	

24F	25B		26D	27D	28B	29H	30C		31B	32F	33B	34C	35E	36G
O	N		T	H	E	I	R		B	O	D	I	E	S

A. The sound a sheep makes
B A A
5 20 10

B. Not in front of
B E H I N D
31 28 9 21 25 33

C. What your body does when it's cold
S H I V E R
23 19 34 11 12 30

D. One of the things you chew with
T O O T H
1 17 6 26 27

E. Curds and _____
W H E Y
18 2 35 4

F. Sound an owl makes
H O O T
13 32 24 7

G. Land at the edge of water
S H O R E
36 8 14 22 3

H. Sick
I L L
29 15 16

page 8 • Mighty Muskox

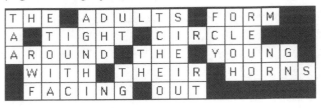

T	H	E		A	D	U	L	T	S		F	O	R	M
A		T	I	G	H	T		C	I	R	C	L	E	
A	R	O	U	N	D		T	H	E		Y	O	U	N	G
	W	I	T	H		T	H	E	I	R		H	O	R	N	S
	F	A	C	I	N	G		O	U	T					

page 9 • Caribou Moves

Answer: MIGRATION

page 10 • Close Up

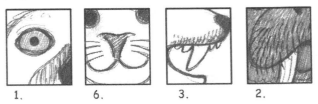

1.   6.   3.   2.

page 10 • Polar Playroom

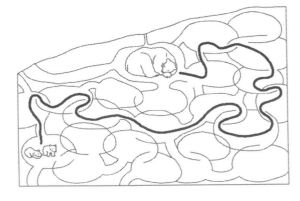

112

page 11 • Flippered Family

Flippered Family Name							
P	I	N	N	I	P	E	D
13	24	11	11	7	13	4	12

What's a perfect pinniped?

A	N		I	D	E	A	L		S	E	A	L
8	3		1	9	5	8	2		6	5	8	2

page 12 • Lots of Lemmings

page 14 • How Many Buses Equal One Shark?

One school bus weighs 5 tons (10,000 divided by 2,000), so one whale shark is equal to three school buses (15 divided by 5).

page 14 • So Big!

SING	THE	DOLPHIN	PIN	LARGEST
BIG	LITTLE	ANIMAL	AT	WOOT
ON	EARTH	COOL	DOWN	JIG
NOODLE	TOO	WIN	IS	TINY
THE	POOL	HOOT	BRING	DIVE
SOON	DEEP	BLUE	PIG	WIG
WING	TENT	AM	WHALE	FOOL

ANSWER: The largest animal on Earth is the blue whale.

A blue whale (at 220 tons) would equal 44 school buses!

page 15 • Water World

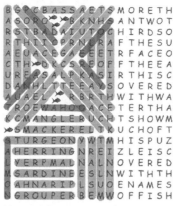

```
BGPCBASSAETSMORETH
ASOPOXBKNHSANTWOT
RSTBADAIUTCHIRDSO
RTHIIOPRNIRAFTHESU
AEUACEGABEETRFACEO
CTHXDKCSREOFFTHEEA
UREXSALPKASIRTHISC
DAMHLTIEEASOVERED
ABAELXRBRTHWITHWA
ROEWAHOACETERTHA
YCMANGLERUCHTSHOWM
XSMACKERELTKUCHOFT
STURGEONYWTMHISPUZ
AHERRINGNREIZLEISC
LYERPMALNALNOVERED
ASARDINEBSLNWITHTH
XAHNARIPLSUOENAMES
GROUPERBEMWOFFISH
```

Unused letters read:
More than two thirds of the surface of the earth is covered with water. That's how much of this puzzle is covered with the names of fish!

page 16 • Create a Fish

Here are some sample "silly fish." Your drawings will probably look very different from these!

1. TRUMPETFISH
2. CLOWNFISH
3. FLAGTAIL

page 16 • Crusty Fellow

Why wouldn't the lobster share his toys?

Answer: He was too shellfish (selfish)!

page 17 • Army of Arms and Funny Family

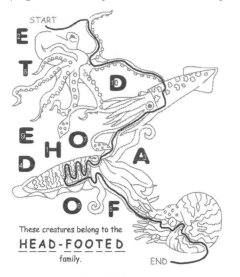

These creatures belong to the
HEAD-FOOTED family.

page 18 • Nice Neigh-bor

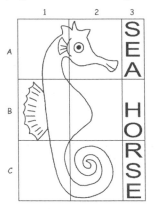

page 19 • Lights, Please!

page 20 • Ocean Hink Pinks

1. What a gilled water animal wants = FISH WISH
2. Letters to a large ocean mammal = WHALE MAIL
3. Little tiny body of water = WEE SEA
4. A great home for a hermit crab = SWELL SHELL
5. Where fish with sharp teeth play = SHARK PARK
6. Flippered sea animal's food = SEAL MEAL
7. Genuine snake-like fish = REAL EEL
8. Metal fish part = TIN FIN
9. Slow moving bunch of mollusks = CLAM JAM
10. Flat shark relative that likes sunlight = DAY RAY

page 20 • Hidden Treasure

WOW! He's big! A giant treasure chest!

page 21 • Where's Dinner?

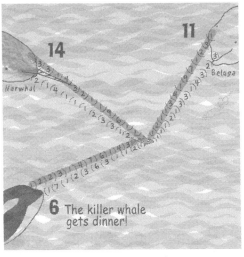

6 The killer whale gets dinner!

page 21 • Who's a Whale?

DOLPHIN

page 22 • Blue Baby

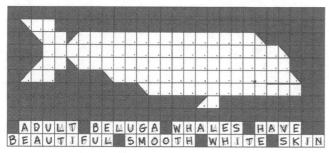

ADULT BELUGA WHALES HAVE BEAUTIFUL SMOOTH WHITE SKIN

page 22 • What Do You Sea?

SEA S H O R E = land that borders the ocean

SEA F O O D = fried clams or baked haddock

SEA L = mammal with flippers instead of feet

SEA P L A N E = vehicle that can land on water

SEA P O R T = a harbor used by ships

SEA S H E L L = hard covering of a clam

SEA S I C K = dizzy from the rolling of a boat

SEA T = something to sit on

SEA W E E D = plant that grows in the sea

page 23 • At the Shore

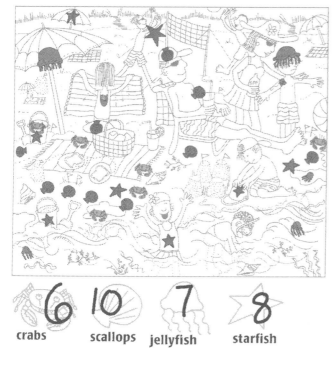

6 crabs **10** scallops **7** jellyfish **8** starfish

page 24 • Home Sweet Habitat

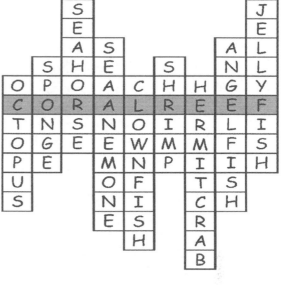

page 26 • Scrambled Eggs

AGRSS _GRASS_
AVELES _LEAVES_
GSEG _EGGS_
TANS _ANTS_
OTROS _ROOTS_
UIRRSQEL _SQUIRREL_

OWEFLRS _FLOWERS_
NEHOY _HONEY_
EDER _DEER_
RBHES _HERBS_
RRIBEES _BERRIES_

SOBIN _BISON_
PHEGORS _GOPHERS_
LBBUS _BULBS_
ZALIRD _LIZARD_
LMOSAN _SALMON_
RBAGAGE _GARBAGE_

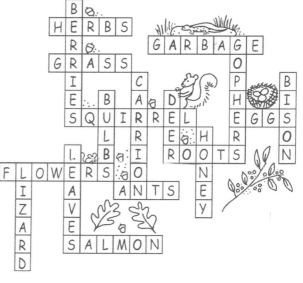

What is "carrion"? The secret message is typed backward and reads "ROTTEN MEAT"

page 27 • **A Mountain What?**

Answer:
The mountain
goat is
really an
ANTELOPE.

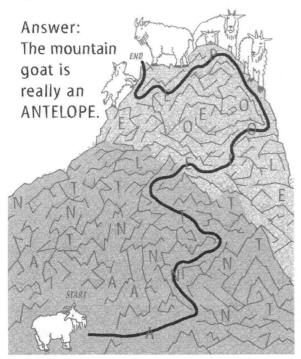

page 28 • **King of the Mountain**

BIGHORN
SHEEP

page 29 • **All Mixed Up**

1. D E W O E R I F =
   <u>D E E R</u> + <u>W O L F</u>
2. R A C O P O C O O S S U N M =
   <u>R A C C O O N</u> + <u>O P O S S U M</u>
3. B E C O A V U G E R A R =
   <u>B E A V E R</u> + <u>C O U G A R</u>
4. S Q U P O R I R R C U P E L I N E =
   <u>S Q U I R R E L</u> + <u>P O R C U P I N E</u>
5. M O O S K U S E N K =
   <u>M O O S E</u> + <u>S K U N K</u>

page 29 • **Lovely Llamas?**

L̶L̶T A H M
A E L̶Y L̶A
M S A L̶L̶M
P A M I A T

They spit!

page 30 • **Where's My Poult?**

ADULT	BABY
mountain lion	kitten
mountain goat	kid
white tailed deer	fawn
beaver	kit
grizzly bear	cub
golden eagle	eaglet
wild turkey	poult
gray wolf	pup

page 31 • **What Do Skunks Have . . . ?**

*What do skunks have that
no other animals have?*

Answer: BABY SKUNKS!

page 32 • Silly Sentences

1. <u>M</u> erry <u>M</u> oose <u>M</u> ake <u>M</u> any <u>M</u> essy <u>M</u> ittens.
2. <u>P</u> orcupine <u>P</u> arents <u>P</u> aint <u>P</u> rickly <u>P</u> ictures.
3. <u>B</u> aby <u>B</u> ears <u>B</u> ake <u>B</u> eautiful <u>B</u> rown <u>B</u> read.
4. <u>F</u> ive <u>F</u> urry <u>F</u> oxes <u>F</u> ry <u>F</u> resh <u>F</u> rankfurters.
5. <u>W</u> eary <u>W</u> olves <u>W</u> heel <u>W</u> ooden <u>W</u> heelbarrows.
6. <u>R</u> idiculous <u>R</u> accoons <u>R</u> ead <u>R</u> obot <u>R</u> iddles.

page 32 • The Scavenger

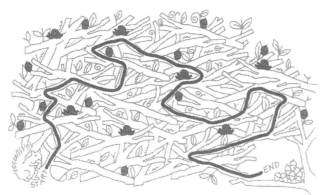

EXTRA FUN Answer: 7 snails, 11 acorns

page 33 • Close Cousins

1.  +L   JACKAL

2. C+  +O+T   COYOTE

3. D+  -R+O   DINGO

page 33 • V.I.M. (Very Important Marmot)

```
E T H E Y F
L A L L L O
G I K E C X
A T O E O N
E A T M Y Y
R A E B O L
A R M O T T
F L O W E S
```

Answer:
They all like to
eat marmots!

page 34 • Yak Math

10	7	3	6	4
-2	+8	-2	+4	-3
8	15	1	10	1

+4	-5	+8	+3	+6
12	10	9	13	7

-7	-6	+3	-5	-4
5	4	12	8	3

+3	+1	-4	-4	+6
8	5	8	4	9

-6	-5	-8	-4	-9
2	0	0	0	0

EXTRA FUN
Answer: a little
more than 307!

Answer: Yaks can climb to
20,000 feet! It's important
to remember that the yaks
don't climb 20,000 all at
once — they already live
high on the mountain.

page 34 • Nest Numbers

# of cards in eight decks	(52 cards per deck) 416
# of keys on eight pianos	(88 keys per piano) 704
# of days in two years	(365 days per year) 730
# of dimes in $200	(10 dimes per dollar) 2,000
# of pennies in six quarters	(25 pennies per quarter) 150

This is how many pounds a big nest can weigh! | **4,000** 2,000 lbs. per ton, or 2 tons!

page 35 • Here Kitty, Kitty?

PANTHER

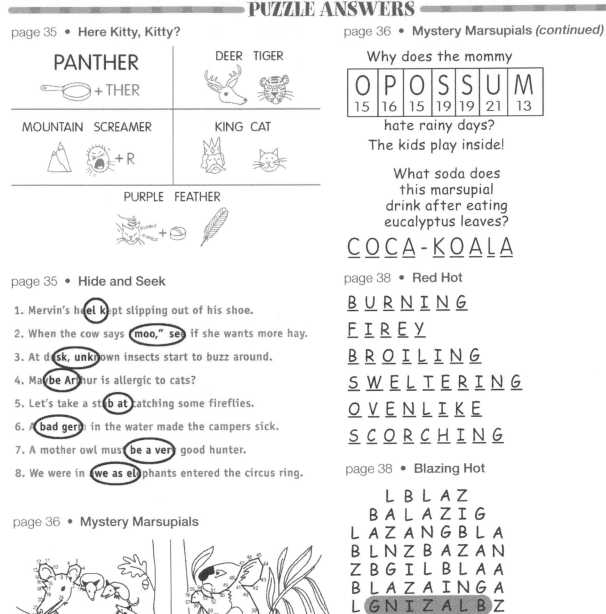

+ THER

DEER TIGER

MOUNTAIN SCREAMER

+ R

KING CAT

PURPLE FEATHER

+

page 35 • Hide and Seek

1. Mervin's he(el k)ept slipping out of his shoe.

2. When the cow says ("moo," se)e if she wants more hay.

3. At du(sk, unk)nown insects start to buzz around.

4. Ma(ybe Ar)thur is allergic to cats?

5. Let's take a sta(b at) catching some fireflies.

6. A (bad germ) in the water made the campers sick.

7. A mother owl must (be a ver)y good hunter.

8. We were in a(we as el)ephants entered the circus ring.

page 36 • Mystery Marsupials

page 36 • Mystery Marsupials *(continued)*

Why does the mommy

O	P	O	S	S	U	M
15	16	15	19	19	21	13

hate rainy days?
The kids play inside!

What soda does
this marsupial
drink after eating
eucalyptus leaves?

C O C A - K O A L A

page 38 • Red Hot

B U R N I N G

F I R E Y

B R O I L I N G

S W E L T E R I N G

O V E N L I K E

S C O R C H I N G

page 38 • Blazing Hot

```
  L B L A Z
 B A L A Z I G
L A Z A N G B L A
B L N Z B A Z A N
Z B G I L B L A A
B L A Z A I N G A
L G N I Z A L B Z
Z A G N B L L
  L A G Z I
```

page 38 • Out of the Heat

D	R	S	H	U	Z	S	H	N	M
E	S	T	I	V	A	T	I	O	N
F	T	U	J	W	B	U	J	P	O

page 39 • Ssssnakes

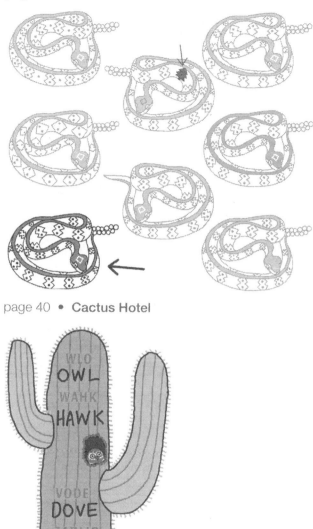

page 40 • Cactus Hotel

WLO
OWL

WAHK
HAWK

VODE
DOVE

ZARLID
LIZARD

RNEW
WREN

SUMOE
MOUSE

ATB
BAT

PIDSER
SPIDER

page 40 • Covered in Sand

SANDWICH

SANDPAPER

SANDMAN

SANDBAG

page 40 • Grains of Sand

1. My aunt (Sand) lives in (San D)iego.

2. Ca(sand)a brought chip(s and)dip.

3. Su(san d)g a hole in the (sand) ox.

page 41 • Leaping Lizards

page 42 • Taxi!

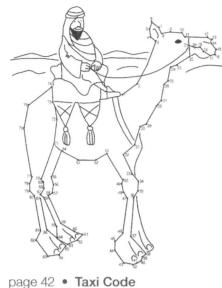

page 42 • Taxi Code

This creature is a

D R O M E D A R Y
4 18 15 13 5 4 1 18 25

or one-humped

C A M E L
3 1 13 5 12

page 43 • Many Meerkats

The total of all the numbers in the picture is 108. Since there are 12 meerkats (including the babies), each meerkat gets 9.

page 44 • Find the Oasis

page 45 • Mystery Monster

Spends much of the day __underground__ **G**
Has a stubby __tail__ that stores fat. **I**
Has strong, wide __claws__. **L**
Is most __active__ at night. **A**

Has __venom__ in glands in its jaw. **M**
Is a __slow__-moving creature. **O**
It should __never__ be approached. **N**
Lives in __tunnels__. **S**
Its bite is painful, but rarely __fatal__. **T**
Eats bird __eggs__, bugs, mice, and lizards. **E**
Has __round__ scales called beads. **R**

page 46 • Small Survivors

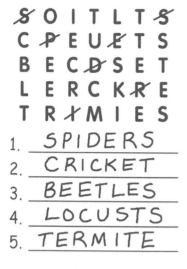

1. __SPIDERS__
2. __CRICKET__
3. __BEETLES__
4. __LOCUSTS__
5. __TERMITE__

page 46 • Small But Deadly

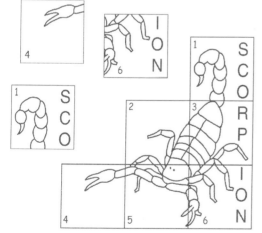

page 47 • Hot Days, Cool Nights

UNDERGROUND

page 47 • Sand Dune Surprise

SAND RAT

page 48 • Beep Beep

page 50 • Why Did the Lion Cross the Grassland?

Answer: To get to the other pride!

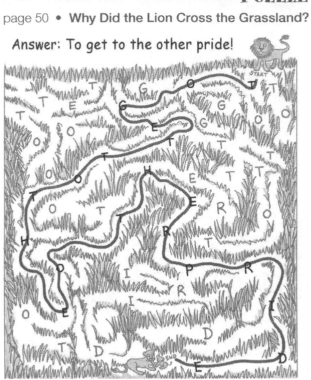

page 51 • Kangaroo Hop

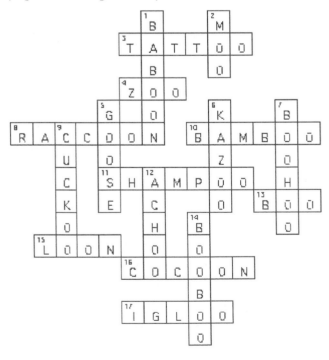

page 52 • What Is It?

Use words from the list to finish this story about a very __strange__ animal. Its name means "little __armored__ one" because it has leathery __bands__ around its body, a long, scaly __tail__, and its face and ears are covered with thick, __bumpy__ skin. When scared, these creatures will jump straight __up__ in the air! Originally from __South America__, this "tiny tank" has moved north. In fact, it is the state mammal of __Texas__!

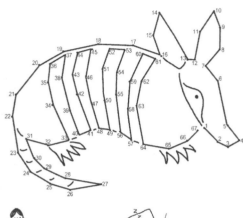

ARMADILLO

page 53 • A World Full of Grass

1. Rae B. Hairy is going to the P R A I R I E.
North America

2. Anna Banana is visiting the S A V A N N A.
Australia

3. Pete Prep will travel to the S T E P P E.
Asia & E. Europe

4. Sam and his compass look for the P A M P A S.
South America

5. Pam Lampost wants to see the C A M P O S.
Equator

6. Lani wants rain when she goes to the P L A I N.
Africa

page 54 • What Do You Get if You Cross a Kangaroo with an Elephant?

	1B Y	2A O	3F U		4E G	5F E	6G T	
7A B	8E I	9F G		10D H	11B O	12C L	13D E	14D S
	15C A	16E L	17G L		18A O	19D V	20G E	21E R
22D A	23B U	24G S	25A T	26F R	27F A	28E L	29C I	30G A

page 55 • Tallest of All

page 55 • Fastest of All

C H E E T A H
3 8 5 5 20 1 8

The code numbers add up to 50. Add 10 more, and that means the cheetah's top speed is 60 miles per hour!

page 56 • You Snooze, You Lose

START

RUN　　STOP　　DOZE　　SMILE　　SWIFT
SPRINT　SPEED　SLEEP　GO　　SCURRY
STAND　HURRY　SCURRY　LAZY　　STOP
DAWDLE　PAUSE　SPRINT　GALLOP　HUSTLE

END

page 56 • Hide and Eat

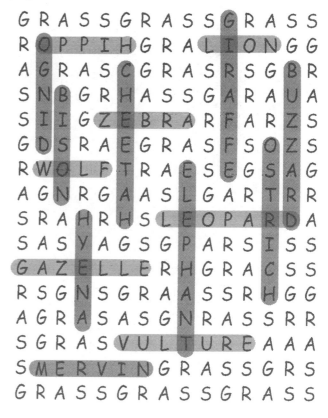

```
G R A S S G R A S S G R A S S
R O P P I H G R A L I O N G G
A G R A S C G R A S R S G B R
S N B G R H A S S G A R A U A
S I I G Z E B R A R F A R Z S
G D S R A E G R A S F S O Z S
R W O L F T R A E S E G S A G
A G N R G A A S L G A R T R R
S R A H R H S L E O P A R D A
S A S Y A G S G P A R S I S S
G A Z E L L E R H G R A C S S
R S G N S G R A A S S R H G G
A G R A S A S G N R A S S R R
S G R A S V U L T U R E A A A
S M E R V I N G R A S S G R S
G R A S S G R A S S G R A S S
```

page 57 • Playing in the Mud

M	U	D		I	S		A	N	I	M	A	L
S	U	N	S	C	R	E	E	N	!		I	T
P	R	O	T	E	C	T	S		T	H	E	I	R
S	K	I	N		A	N	D		K	E	E	P	S
I	T		M	O	I	S	T	.				

page 58 • **Marvelous Meadowlark**

KANSAS STATE BIRD

K S A A T A E R D B
N S T A S I

page 58 • **Smooch!**

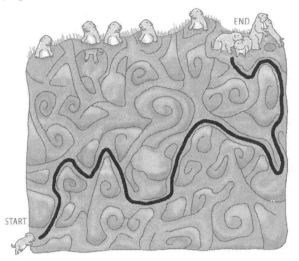

START

END

page 59 • **The Watering Hole**

page 59 • **Designed to Disappear**

You might think you see nine gray dots. This pattern is an optical illusion. It tricks the eye into thinking there are gray dots where the white lines cross each other. If you look directly at the dot, you will notice that it disappears! That's because there really are no gray dots at all.

page 60 • **Hop to It!**

50	130	80	10	90
90	30	40	110	70
110	70	10	200	50
50	90	210	230	60
210	10	80	140	130
50	160	70	30	10
10	210	20	90	50
120	40	30	110	70

page 60 • **Look Fast**

page 62 • **Going Up**

page 64 • **We Need Rain!**

B A T

A N T

C H I M P A N Z E E

C R O C O D I L E

H U M M I N G B I R D

I G U A N A

J A G U A R

L E O P A R D

L I Z A R D

O R A N G U T A N

P A R R O T

S N A I L

S N A K E

T A R A N T U L A

T E R M I T E

T I G E R

F R O G S

T O U C A N

page 64 • **We Need Rain!** *(continued)*

```
T O R R A P W H Y D I D
D T H I G U A N A E G O
R T O U C A N R I B A T
I L L D R A Z I L A S T
B L I C K H I S H E A D
G E E Z N A P M I H O
N O T F R O G S H R O R
I P U G R H T H E N U O
M A M S E B R E L A T C
M R L N G A T O J T E O
U D S A I E E A I U R D
H F I I T T G H A G M I
A N T L D U S T O N I L
P P E D A R A I N A T E
I N G R E K A N S R E Y
T A R A N T U L A O E T
```

Leftover letters:

Why did the gorilla stick his head through the umbrella?

To see if it had stopped raining yet!

page 65 • **Big Beautiful Bills**

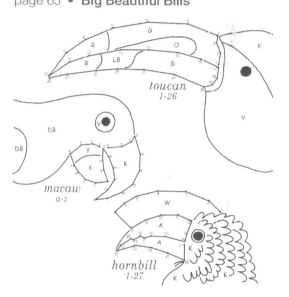

toucan
1-26

macaw
a-z

hornbill
1-27

page 66 • **Biiiiiig Snake**

made of tin	C	A	N
before two	O	N	E
girl's nickname	P	A	T
frozen water	I	C	E
cat chaser	D	O	G
picnic insect	A	N	T
not even	O	D	D
lunch sack	B	A	G

page 66 • **Super Bug**

Of course, everyone's answer will be different depending on what they weigh. Let's try the formula assuming that you weigh 100 pounds. If you were as strong as a rhinoceros beetle, you could lift 85,000 pounds! That's forty-two and a half tons! Now, if you weighed 100 pounds, but were as strong as an elephant, you could lift only 25 pounds. That's the same as 5 bags of sugar. You can see that ounce for ounce the rhinoceros beetle deserves the title "strongest creature in the world"!!

page 67 • Slow as a Sloth

```
L  D  K  E
I  O  Z  Y
P  A  L  Y
```

1. L A Z Y
2. I D L E
3. P O K Y

page 67 • In Hiding

page 68 • Crocodile Bites

page 69 • Lonely Lemur

MADAGASCAR

page 69 • Rainforest

an, as, in, on, no, it, if, is, of, so, ant, art, ran, fan, tan, tin, sin, fin, for, ore, nit, fit, sit, far, for, son, sat, fat, are, ton, tone, raft, fast, fort, fair, sort, fine, tore, fore, sore, rant, roar, rest, soar, fist, soft, sift, rare, stare, store, stain, saint, feast, frost, front, often, reason, soften, strain, refrain, treason

page 70 • Who Am I?

JAGUAR

page 70 • Tiny Farmers

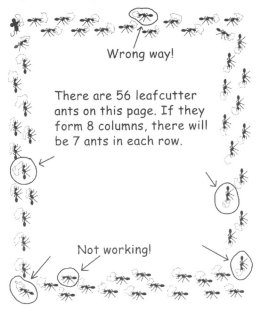

Wrong way!

There are 56 leafcutter ants on this page. If they form 8 columns, there will be 7 ants in each row.

Not working!

page 71 • Breezy Butterflies

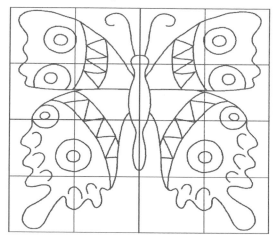

page 71 • Batty for Fruit

G F B

1. F I G

2. M A N G O

3. B A N A N A

page 72 • Barrel of Monkeys?

1. Where's a good place for monkeys to swim?
   In the **Chimpan Sea**

2. What's a monkey's favorite Christmas carol?
   Jungle Bells

3. What does a monkey learn in kindergarten?
   His **Ape B C's**

4. When do monkeys fall from the sky?
   During Ape-ril showers

5. What kind of monkey can fly?
   A **hot air baboon**

6. What's a monkey's favorite cookie?
   Chocolate chimp

page 74 • Above the Barn

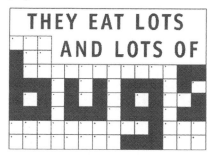

THEY EAT LOTS AND LOTS OF bugs

page 74 • In the Barn

DONKEY COW GOAT TURKEY CHICKEN HORSE SHEEP GOOSE

page 75 • Cat and Mouse

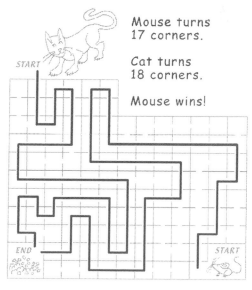

Mouse turns 17 corners.

Cat turns 18 corners.

Mouse wins!

START END START

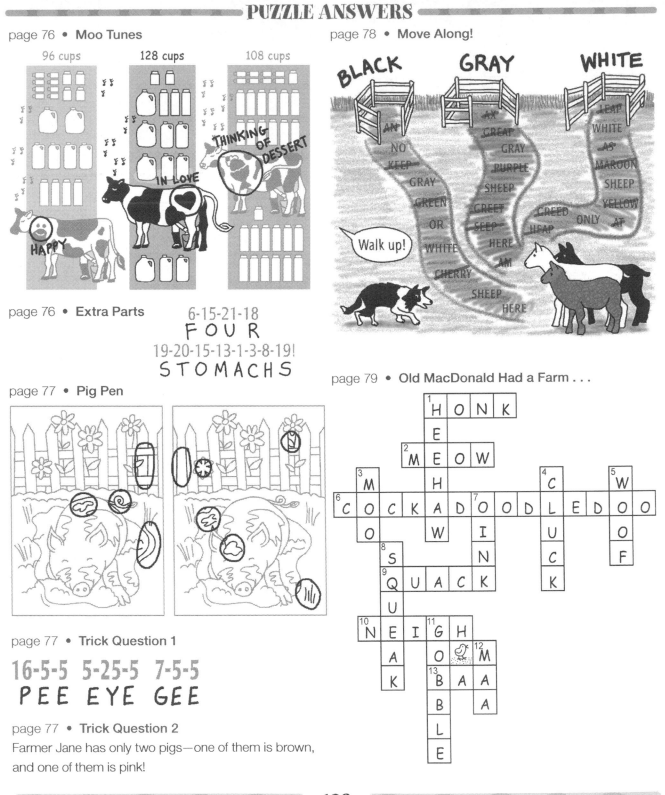

page 76 • **Moo Tunes**

96 cups   128 cups   108 cups

THINKING OF DESSERT

IN LOVE

HAPPY

page 76 • **Extra Parts**

6-15-21-18
F O U R
19-20-15-13-1-3-8-19!
S T O M A C H S

page 77 • **Pig Pen**

page 77 • **Trick Question 1**

16-5-5   5-25-5   7-5-5
P E E   E Y E   G E E

page 77 • **Trick Question 2**

Farmer Jane has only two pigs—one of them is brown, and one of them is pink!

page 78 • **Move Along!**

BLACK   GRAY   WHITE

Walk up!

page 79 • **Old MacDonald Had a Farm . . .**

page 79 • Old MacDonald Had a Farm . . . (cont'd)

Across
1. G O O S E
2. C A T
6. R O O S T E R
9. D U C K
10. H O R S E
13. S H E E P

Down
1. D O N K E Y
3. C O W
4. C H I C K E N
5. D O G
7. P I G
8. M O U S E
11. T U R K E Y
12. G O A T

page 79 • Lawn Mowers

BARN	YARD	STICK	SOME	BODY	BUILD
HOME	WORK	SHOP	HAND	GUARD	ONE
WORK	OUT	LIFT	OFF	RAIL	HEAD
BOOK	SIDE	HOME	BEAT	ROAD	SIDE

page 80 • Chicken Scratch

There are 10 of this kind of chicken.

There are 8 of this kind of chicken.

There are 10 of this kind of chicken.

There are 5 of this kind of chicken.

There is only one of this kind of chicken.

page 81 • Nobody Here But Us Chickens

1. An owl makes this sound, not a chicken = H O O T
2. When it's full, chickens can see at night = M O O N
3. Chickens can't read this = B O O K
4. Chickens love to eat this = F O O D
5. Time of day when chickens eat lunch = N O O N
6. The top part of the chicken coop = R O O F
7. Most chicken coops are made from this = W O O D

page 81 • Barnyard Hink Pinks

1. Escaped fowl with long neck= L O O S E   G O O S E
2. Baby cow's giggle = C A L F   L A U G H
3. Quacker that can't move = S T U C K   D U C K
4. Baby sheep blocking the creek = L A M B   D A M
5. Being bumped by a young horse = C O L T   J O L T
6. Canoe for a kid's dad = G O A T   B O A T

EXTRA FUN: The last Hink Pink has <u>three</u> rhyming words.
7. Large swine hair = B I G   P I G   W I G

page 82 • If the Shoe Fits

H	O	R	S	E	S	H	O	E	S	
	A	R	E		A		S	I	G	N
	O	F		G	O	O	D			
L	U	C	K	!						

page 82 • What Kind of Allergy . . .

page 84 • Where Is Everybody?

WE WENT TO THE MOOVIES

page 86 • Here, Rover?

~~Buddy~~ ~~Molly~~
~~Bailey~~ ~~Sadie~~
~~Jake~~ ~~Sam~~
(Max) ~~Maggie~~
~~Nicky~~ ~~Coco~~

page 83 • Funny Farm

page 86 • Hungry Herd
Neudge eats first.

page 87 • Perfect Parakeet

page 87 • Sounds Like . . .

bark, growl, hiss, meow, purr, squeak, squeal, tweet, whistle, yelp, yowl

page 88 • Kate's Kittens

page 89 • Pets on the Run

A rug = C A R P E T

Small = P E T I T E

Part of a flower = P E T A L

Hand toy = P U P P E T

Fancy slip = P E T T I C O A T

Gasoline = P E T R O L E U M

Castle wall = P A R A P E T

Musical instrument = T R U M P E T

Turn into stone = P E T R I F Y

Summer flower = P E T U N I A

page 90 • I Love My Pet

Everybody will have a totally different story! Here's ours.

I have a very <u>SLINKY</u> pet named <u>RUFUS</u>.
descriptive word / funny name

He is <u>3½</u> feet tall and weighs <u>137</u> pounds. He is a beautiful
number / number

shade of <u>YELLOW</u>, with <u>PURPLE</u> <u>POLKA DOTS</u>
color / different color / pattern (stripes. etc.)

on his <u>ELBOWS</u>. I keep him in a <u>BASKET</u>
body part / container

in the <u>BATHTUB</u>. <u>RUFUS</u> loves
place in the house / same name used on line one

to eat <u>MACARONI AND CHEESE</u>! I need to <u>JUMP</u>
food / action word

him around the block <u>23</u> times a day. I love my pet!
number

page 90 • The Dog Walker

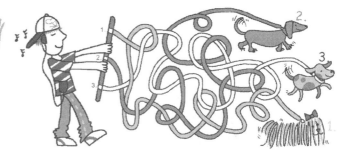

page 91 • Furry Friends

• There are nine mice (4 white, 5 gray), and 11 gerbils.

• All the guinea pigs and rabbits do not have the same pattern. The guinea pig at the bottom of the page has a white head and hindquarters, and a dark middle. All other guinea pigs and rabbits have dark head and hindquarters and a white middle.

• There is only one hamster.

page 92 • Silly Sentences

1. <u>H</u>arry's <u>h</u>airy <u>h</u>amster <u>h</u>id <u>h</u>amburgers.
2. <u>P</u>enny's <u>p</u>retty <u>p</u>arrot <u>p</u>erched <u>p</u>erpendicular.
3. <u>F</u>red's <u>f</u>inest <u>f</u>ishes <u>f</u>ixed <u>f</u>ive <u>f</u>ences.
4. <u>D</u>avid's <u>d</u>irty <u>d</u>og <u>d</u>rew <u>d</u>ancing <u>d</u>inosaurs.
5. <u>C</u>ara's <u>c</u>razy <u>c</u>at <u>c</u>ooked <u>c</u>old <u>c</u>ucumbers.
6. <u>S</u>imon's <u>S</u>even <u>S</u>nakes <u>S</u>ipped <u>S</u>weet <u>S</u>odas.
7. <u>I</u>sabel's <u>i</u>tchy <u>i</u>guana <u>i</u>gnored <u>i</u>nsects.

page 92 • Pet Hair Is Everywhere

SOFA　　SHORTS
CHAIR　　JACKET
DRESS　　T-SHIRT
SUIT　　SWEATER
PANTS　　BEDSPREAD

page 93 • What Pet Did Annie Get?

page 94 • Too Close!

1. PIG
2. CAT
3. SEAHORSE
4. FISH
5. MOUSE
6. PARAKEET
7. RABBIT
8. DOG
9. SNAKE

page 94 • Funny Fish

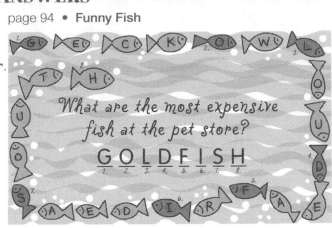

What are the most expensive fish at the pet store?

G O L D F I S H
1. 2. 3. 4. 5. 6. 7. 8.

page 95 • First Fish

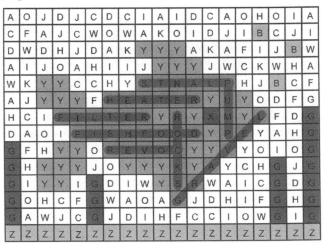

page 96 • Listen to Your Pet!

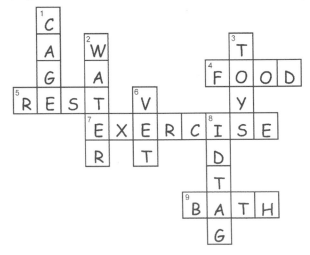

Across:
4. FOOD
5. REST
7. EXERCISE
9. BATH

Down:
1. CAGE
2. WATER
3. TOY
6. VET
8. DIET

page 96 • Dog Talk

The word BARK has been added after every letter in the answer! If you remove all the BARKs, the answer reads "Put him in the back yard!"

page 98 • Once Upon a Time . . .

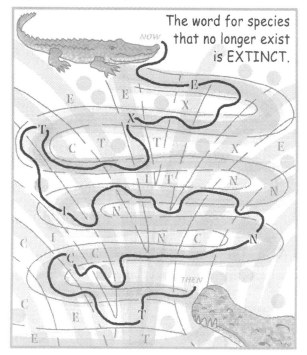

The word for species that no longer exist is EXTINCT.

page 99 • We Love Dinosaurs!

page 99 • Animals from the Past

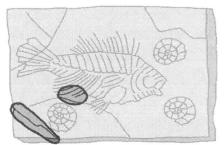

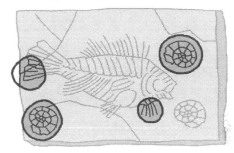

page 100 • Going Backward

8-1-2-9-20-1-20 4-5-19-20-18-21-3-20-9-15-14
h a b i t a t d e s t r u c t i o n

16 - 15 - 12 - 12 - 21 - 20 - 9 - 15 - 14
p o l l u t i o n

page 100 • Moving Forward

KOZMGRMT GIVVH
PLANTING TREES

MZGRLMZO KZIPH
NATIONAL PARKS

page 101 • Butterfly Blues

page 101 • Butterfly Count

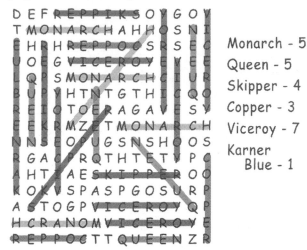

```
D E F R E P P I K S O Y G O V
T M O N A R C H A H H O S N I
C H R H R E P P O O S R S E C
U O E G V I C E R O Y E V E E
Q P S M O N A R C H C I U O R
B U P Y H T N T G T H I C Q O
R E I O T O E R A G A V E S Y
E K R K M Z E T M O N A R C H
N N S E O P U G S N S H O O S
R G A C R Q T H T E T Y P C I
A H T I A E S K I P P E R O O
K O K V S P A S P G O S U R P
A S T O G P V I C E R O Y Q P
H C R A N O M V I C E R O Y E
R E P P O C T T Q U E E N Z R
```

Monarch - 5

Queen - 5

Skipper - 4

Copper - 3

Viceroy - 7

Karner
Blue - 1

page 102 • Gentle Giants

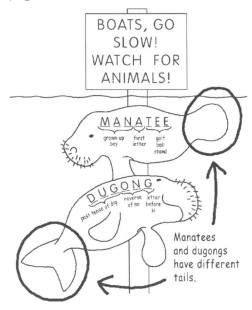

BOATS, GO SLOW! WATCH FOR ANIMALS!

MANATEE
grown-up boy / first letter / golf ball stand

DUGONG
past tense of dig / reverse of no / letter before H

Manatees and dugongs have different tails.

page 103 • Save the Tiger!

KEEP OUT! THIS IS

page 104 • Poor Rhino

```
1G  2C  3L      4G  5A  6H  7K  8B
T   H   E       H   O   R   N   S
    9C  10I 11L     12E 13L 14H 15C
    A   R   E       U   S   E   D
    16K 17J     18A 19H 20B 21F
    T   O       M   A   K   E
22H 23I 24F 25B 26B 27G 28G 29F
M   E   D   I   C   I   N   E
30I 31J 32H     33L 34K 35E 36F 37A 38F
A   N   D       D   A   G   G   E   R
    39E 40D 41A 42D 43A 44C 45D
    H   A   N   D   L   E   S
```

A. Sour fruit
L E M O N
43 37 18 5 41

B. To be ill
S I C K
8 25 26 20

C. Body part under a hat
H E A D
2 44 9 15

D. Unhappy
S A D
45 40 42

E. Squeeze with your arms
H U G
39 12 35

F. Selfish desire for more
G R E E D
36 38 21 29 24

G. Skinny
T H I N
1 4 27 28

H. Picture in your sleep
D R E A M
32 6 14 19 22

I. To be
A R E
30 10 23

J. Opposite of yes
N O
31 17

K. Light brown color
T A N
16 34 7

L. What a plant grows from
S E E D
13 3 11 33

page 104 • Gotcha!

He gave the rhino a bell instead!

page 105 • Island Attraction

TORTOISE

TOROISET
move second T to end

TUROISET
change first O to U

TOURISET
move O before U

TOURIST
delete E

page 105 • **Say Cheese!**

page 106 • **There's No Place Like Home**

defend · neglect · destroy · secure · SUPPORT · care for · FAIL · guard · ruin · harm · ignore · burn · SHIELD · preserve · uproot · save · damage · shelter · rescue · watch over · HELP · pollute

page 106 • **Sad Panda/Glad Panda**

page 107 • **What Can I Do?**

```
E3Q4   I385Y,
DEAR  KEITH,
8   297QE  08I3   5P
I   WOULD  LIKE  TO
Y3Q*   QH8JQQW.
HELP  ANIMALS.
8      IH92      5YQ5
I    KNOW    THAT
8W    6974    U9G.
IS    YOUR    JOB.
*Q3QW3
PLEASE
53QQ    J3    3943!
TELL    ME    MORE!
Y3Q5Y34
HEATHER
```

page 107 • **Be Like Me!**

C	= the third one
O	= one before P
N	= between M and O
S	= two after Q
E	= the fifth one
R	= one before S
V	= between U and W
A	= the first one
T	= one after S
I	= between H and J
O	= three before R
N	= two after L
I	= three after F
S	= between R and T
T	= two before V

page 108 • **Home to Us All**

page 110 • **Now Where Did I See That . . . ?**

1. Mighty Muskox   2. CrustyFellow   3. Mystery Marsupial

4. Find the Oasis   5. Hop To It!   6. Going Up

7. Where is Everybody?   8. The Hungry Herd   9. Butterfly Blues